The Mixtape

Marcia Monique Miller- Spence

TABLE OF CONTENTS

DEDICATION

We dedicate the MixTape to Marcia Miller Spence, the mother of my children, who passed away on March 26, 2020. The greatest gift you ever gave me was our two beautiful children. Thank you so much for making me a father and giving me something to hold on to now that you are gone. They will be reminded every day how much you love them. You will be their first thought in the morning and their last thought at night. With your passing, the road has become tougher. Through every trial, disappointment, and challenge, you have strengthened and blessed us. We feel your presence now. We feel your support. As we endeavor to move forward with whatever God has planned for us, I know that with Briana and Jacob, we will move forward together! Although you are gone, your love, strength, and courage inspire us daily. You remain the wind beneath our wings.

ABOUT THE AUTHOR

Christopher Spence is an educator, filmmaker, author and father.

He is the author of YA books that include SnowBall Brothers4Life, Ice Cold and The Adventures of Bobby Allen. His film credits include Teammates, SkinGames, Football's Pioneering Duo, Silence the Violence, and Jail or Yale: Young, Black and Out of Options?

CHAPTER 1

Coach Taylor looks at the football team standing shoulder to shoulder in the locker room. With determination written across their faces, it seems like they are ready for show time and the crushing of their opponents.

"Winning is simply a mindset," the coach exclaims as he starts his pre-game speech. "A mindset, however, that is only comes from preparation and focus. It's not about talent, it's about effort. Effort will get you the win when you have the heart of a lion. Effort will carry the day when everyone expects you to give up. Effort will pick you up when you have been knocked down.

The coach pauses before continuing, "Winning is the reward you receive when you have put in the hard work when no one is watching! Winning is for champion attitudes and champion hearts! If you throw me to the wolves, know that I will return leading the pack! It only takes one moment to decide you are going to be a winner! One moment is all it takes! One winning moment like today's game."

"It only takes one moment to make a decision! One moment to say no! To say never again!

Never again will I settle! Never again will I accept anything but my best effort! One moment to be strong! One moment to separate myself from the rest! Winning is simply a mindset. A mindset however that is only developed by outstanding individuals! Outwork your competition. If you outwork, your opponent day in and day out, you will beat him come game day! There is no question. But you have to have commitment and discipline, to be better, day in and day out. Always outworking your opponent! One more rep, one more set, one more mile! That is what it takes to get the edge! Winning is what happens when deep down inside, you are driven to succeed! Winning is what happens when your desire to win is greater than your fear of failure! Winning is what happens when your 'why' is bigger than your opponent's 'why'! When your hunger is greater! When your heart and soul says, we got this! I won't settle! I deserve better, success is mine! And I will take what is mine. Sometimes it's gonna be hard. Sometimes it might even seem impossible. But remember, anything is possible if you don't give up! If you stay in the game, hang in there give yourself a shot. It is possible! Forget everything else. … We get one opportunity today, one chance at to hoist that trophy to lay our foundation to leave our legacy. If you put your effort and concentration into playing to your potential, I don't care what the scoreboard says at the end of the game. In my book, we're gonna be winners!

"Yeah!" the team shouts in union as they head towards the field, "Go Cougars!"

***

"Cougars Win! Cougars Win! Cougars Win!" the stands echo with a hundred elated voices.

While the team celebrates their win, a commentator's voice crackles to life over the loudspeaker, "Coach Taylor has to be proud with the way his team played with so much adversity surrounding the team. In particular the play of All American student, athlete and quarterback, Dre Banks, who truly has a one of kind generational talent."

A second commentator adds, "That's right Parker, he's an honor roll student with a cannon of an arm and the speed of a gazelle. He really can do it all. Today, he threw for four touchdowns and ran for another two."

"Let's not forget the others because in football you can't do it on your own," the first commentator replies.

"Absolutely, and that means senior tight end, Noah Reynolds who was over a hundred yards receiving today for the 12th consecutive game and leaves the Cougar program as the all-time leading receiver. He played today with a heavy heart after the recent tragic loss of his sister."

"The courage of this young man is something to behold. And then there's Carlos Fuentes, arguably the most underrated yet dependable receiver in the city despite those soft hands of his. Today, he was Dre's favorite receiver in almost every third in long situation," Parker says.

"And what about that defense? Coach's bend but don't break scheme has worked to perfection. They have been led by the man in the middle, linebacker Kobe Briggs, who is such a disruptive influence out there with four sacks and pick-six to go along with his eighteen tackles, and not forgetting that he, of course, is the son of Bo Briggs, perhaps the greatest linebacker this city has ever seen."

As the two commentators provide the audience in the stands a little insight to the players, the team heads towards the locker room where their coach is waiting to congratulate them.

"That was a great win out there today!" Coach Taylor pats some of the team members on the back as they enter.

The spirit the team shares is almost tangible and if visible, could be seen bouncing off the walls.

"Let's keep this going, boys!" the coach smiles. "Before you all get yourself cleaned up, I would like to say "I am sure you'd all want to get back home to your parents and enjoy a little celebration within limits I assume… enjoy this special moment that comes from a shared commitment to play a role while doing it together that's what you remember not your stats or your prestige but the relationships and the achievement that you created as a team.

I would like to thank the parents of the Cougar players for raising such tremendous young men, developing winners on the field, off the field, through perseverance, character, and mostly love. It's been that kind of a team. It's beyond culture. It's a brotherhood. Parents, what they've poured into these young men from such an early age. Esteeming them when they're young and all the practices and everything they drove them to and took them to. Just the support and love that they give them, however if this is the greatest thing that ever happens to you, I'm going to be disappointed, let this be a catalyst for future greatness. They say you either change your dreams or change your habits, and I damn sure wasn't going to change my dreams. I'm glad you didn't change yours either.

You are champions! Be safe! Be smart!

CHAPTER 2

While finishing up in the locker room, Noah Reynolds decides to walk home. Walking always helped him clear his mind and gave him the chance to think.

He always considered himself lucky. He was part of a close knit family who seemed to have each other's best interests at heart. Having such a wonderful family was a blessing and he seemed like a guy with a bright future - full of enthusiasm, passion and energy. A brilliant guy like him could achieve anything in his life with such high motivations and ambitions.

Noah was an intriguing and intellectual guy and from a young age, he excelled in school. His parents believed in him and had faith that their child was very great with a high level of intellect although their son was somewhat introverted. Despite that, he was an athlete and a great football player.

Apart from that, he was very caring towards his sister Nicki, who was a girl of great potential and from a very young age, seemed keen on cheerleading. Noah loved his sister and always found her to be a blessing for him. He felt relaxed around her and they had a special bond.

"Let's play football, Nicki," Noah usually asked.

"Okay sure. Let's play but no cheating!" Nicki said even though there were other things she would prefer to do.

Noah's father was his inspiration. He wanted to follow his footsteps. All the things he wanted in his life were fulfilled by his father, a guy who was very generous and considerate about others. Like Noah, his father was a man that loved football.

Noah remembered what it was like to sit beside his father on the couch watching football teams bring their best to the game. Although Noah was very young, he would carry those precious memories with his father with him through his entire life. Noah's father loved to discuss the game with his son.

"And that, my son, is what being a sports fan is all about. You're very young, and you don't understand all this, but you just witnessed a very big event. It's not quite as big as some people say, of course. I have already heard one person say that it is the greatest win in the sport history. Of course, it is not. This team has won you know. There have been bigger games. But we beat a very good team, with very good individual players, in a college competition. So it is very big," he would say. "Yes, I know what you are thinking. The media hype that surrounds these power five teams is ridiculous.

Noah looked at his father with admiration although he didn't quite understand everything his father was saying, "Great football game today?"

"Indeed," his father continued. "But, as I was saying, this is what being a fan of sport is all about. Not all days are as good as this one. You have already sat through too many grim losses. But that is what you must do to be a true fan. You cannot just appear for the wins. You must suffer through the losses, to truly savor the wins. And tonight is a time to savor. The entire team played magnificently. I have no complaints tonight. The defense held a very strong team.

Noah smiled, "I love you Dad."

"Yes," Noah's father replied. "I am your Dad, and I love you above all others. There is no one near you. But I confess I have paternal feelings for that Tom Brady. I have only watched him since his Michigan days, but I feel like we have watched him blossom from a boy with promise to a man who dominates football games. Never mind his goals, although he took them with the cool of an assassin. But note, instead, how he dominated the game from beginning to end, how he calmly drove his time down the field from the first minute to the last. I admire him, not just because I have backed him for so long, but because he has grown and transformed into something else. He has become the greatest player to ever play the game."

He paused and looked at Noah, "Of course I will not overlook the other members of the squad. They played as a team today, and I am proud of all of them. Our defense kept them in the game. And the coaching. You know my thoughts on the Great Man-Bill Belichick. However he prepared them in the first half, it worked. They handled a team that, in theory, had superior talent.

"Do you want to watch something else?" Noah asked, not knowing the seriousness of his father's words.

"Or we can go throw the football outside!" Noah suggested.

"Absolutely, son," Noah's father said while deep in thought. "It is a simple game. Just men throwing and catching a ball around, trying to get to the endzone. So simple and so complex. And yet it brings us so much joy, this simple act. We suffer and suffer, and agonize and scream, and in its only a game. I'm just glad I was able to watch it with you. You've never been to a SuperBowl. And therein lays the true beauty and power of football, the power to bring a father and a son together, to watch and cheer a team that plays a game thousands and thousands of miles away. You will understand this all much better when you are older, my son; for now, I am just glad we could be together to watch this."

Noah listened to the melody his father's voice made while he talked without saying another word.

"I guess I am being silly talking to you like this," Noah's father sighed. You are still just a baby. I just like talking to you. What could I expect you to say?"

Yes, the Reynolds household seemed like the perfect family… With the exception of Tim Reynolds. He was exactly the opposite Noah and his father. Tim Reynolds, Noah's uncle, was a cunning character and from a very young age, Noah simply couldn't get himself to like his uncle. In fact, no one in his family quite liked Tim much. At times, he would arrive unannounced during dinner and demand a plate of food from Nancy, Noah's mother.

Tim, unlike Noah's father, was living a life full of badness and was a guy who had committed several crimes and was involved in many dirty dealings. He was an alcoholic and would smoke pot and weed anytime he wanted. He also dabbled in many petty crimes to make some money. He had managed to forge a bad look for himself as all the people in the neighborhood snickered whenever he turned up on his brother's doorstep. Everyone around him felt danger and was afraid to contact him as he had been in and out of jail. Noah had even heard some of the neighbors say that he had some bodies. He did not have any feelings for elder or younger ones either. His appearance said it all.

Whenever Tim showed up at the Reynolds' household, Noah and his sister were told to go to their room.

Tim's rowdy and drunk voice could be heard throughout the house, no matter where Noah huddled. Although Noah was young at the time, he understood that his uncle usually demanded money from his father and the more Noah's dad refused, the more Tim would push. Nancy would let the bickering between her husband and Tim continue until he sent his plate of food crashing to the floor. Noah had always silently observed the family feuds from the top of the staircase.

At seeing Tim boil over, Nancy would throw a few dollar bills at Tim from the jar she kept in the kitchen. With tears in her eyes, she begged her husband to see him out and let the fight rest.

Late at night, after Nancy had put the kids to bed and assured them their uncle meant no harm, Noah would hear his parents talk in hushed voices over cups of tea in the kitchen.

"It cannot go on like this," Noah's dad would say. "He cannot get away with this every time. You know he uses the money for dope. And he knows that every time he gets angry enough, you'll do anything to get him out, even if it means grabbing money from the savings jar."

"What do you want me to do? He is a dangerous man, you said so yourself. I would rather have him take our money than threaten you or the kids… or worse…" Nancy sighed.

"He cannot come in here and take our money. I love my kids and I do not want to hurt them but what I am earning it is for my kids and you… Who the hell is he to do this… All the time you stop me… My brother is going to be the end of me. How long has this been going on? Five years? Seven years? He won't ever change. He is a junkie and there is nothing I can do to help him. I have tried. You know how hard I have tried…" Noah's father would think aloud.

To Noah, not much of what they said made much sense to him. All he knew was that every time he passed his uncle in the house, he would get chills down his spine. From the corner of his eye, he could always see his uncle staring at him with a strange smile on his face. To Noah, it felt like he was some sort of prey and his uncle was the predator…

But as the years sped past, Noah had learned to keep two faces - one he showed to the world - a happy and generous and one where he was very sad and suffering. And when one suffers from that, there is a great reason behind it and that reason was not obvious to others. Even his parents had noticed it. He wanted to share the things his suffering with his parents but he could not because of the embarrassment and humiliation he thought he would face.

This burden had made him change. He was not that happy go lucky guy anymore. He lost his goodwill and he always remembered those moments which had now turned him into a hollow guy.

To avoid the painful events, he started drinking and was attracted to negative experiences all the time.

Whenever Tim came over, he felt like he was a useless guy who couldn't do anything to defend himself and his family against him.

Inside, he was hurting, assaulted and heartbroken, where he was forced to shut his mouth for all the things that have happened to him. He was feeling shameful inside and wanted to run away to avoid facing everyone as he was not able to maintain eye contact with his parents. Whenever he heard his uncle in the house, his body started shivering and sweating…

At age 16, Noah had become somewhat used to the fact that his uncle dropped by every once in a while to cause havoc and demand cash. Although his mother had made it clear that he would not interfere in his father and uncle's disagreements, Noah couldn't help but feel a deep sense of anger and annoyance with Tim. From what he had heard over the past couple of years, his uncle had a slew of charges against him. Assuming the worst, Noah always ensured that Nicki, aged 14 at the time, stayed out of his way when he visited their home. He didn't want her to meet the same fate he already did…

Seeing his father's continued disappointment in him grow, Noah felt the need to come clean with his dad. His parents were under the impression that he was rebelling against life and experimented with drugs and alcohol as an excuse. Noah was sure his mother thought he was following in his uncle's footsteps. But to Noah, that was not the case. It was because of what his uncle had done to him that he was rebelling against life. He didn't know what else to do. But when looking at his father's expression when Noah came home with yet another girl he had just met at a football game, he knew that he had to reach out to someone; anyone who'd listen and perhaps help.

"Dad," Noah had said one afternoon as he was getting his football gear together in the kitchen. "There is something I'd like to talk to you about…"

"Sure, son. Do you think we'd be able to talk about it in the car? Your mother and Nicki went out to run some errands. I thought it would be great if I could come and watch your game today. What do you think?"

Noah reluctantly agreed and cleared his throat before continuing, "Sure. But it's kind of a… big thing…"

"It better not be another one of the drunken brawls that got you into trouble. I told you that I won't tolerate it anymore. I know there is something else going on but if you don't talk, I can't help…" Noah's father said.

While walking to the car, Noah sighed, "Yes, well… That is what I wanted to talk to you about…"

As they drove into the street, his father looked at him, "What is it, son? There is something you've been carrying around with you for years. I want to help. You know I do."

"I…" Noah hung his head.

He had been thinking about the right words he was going to say for months now. He knew exactly what to say. But for some reason, the words didn't want to leave his mouth. He couldn't, no matter how hard he tried.

Come on! Say it! Uncle Tim has made feel . Say it! Noah shouted at himself inwardly.

"Well?" His father said, anticipating what his son had on his heart.

"Nothing… It's nothing…" Noah mumbled and looked out the window. Coward… he scolded himself.

Noah's father seemed disappointed and said nothing. He had thought his son would have enough courage to open up to him. But from experience, he knew that pushing Noah would only drive him further away.

The rest of the trip went by in silence as Noah plucked up the little courage he had left. After the game, he would tell his father. That would be best. As soon as the game was over, he would tell his father what had happened.

"Good luck out there!" Noah's father said as he dropped his son near the locker room. "See you after the game!"

Noah nodded and headed towards a group of guys about to get their football gear on.

On the field, Noah could see his father sitting on the faded blue stands. He felt grateful to have a dad that loved him, no matter what. But he didn't know what would happen after he came clean about his secret. Would his father still love him? Would he reject him?

These questions ran around in Noah's mind as the game began. Only when dropped the first catch did he switch his mind to football mode; a place where nothing else mattered and the opposing team was the only obstacle standing in front of him and victory.

As half time approached, Noah noticed his uncle sitting alongside his father. For a split second, he froze. It seemed like the two men were fighting about something, which was not unusual where Tim was involved.

Suddenly Tim and Noah's father stood up and left the stands, still seemingly involved in a heated argument.

As the second half of the game started, neither Noah's father nor his uncle was anywhere to be seen. Noah closed his mind off to the trouble his family faced and lost himself in the game; another game his team won.

"Noah?" the coach called when the team was celebrating their win in the locker room right after the game.

"Yes, coach?" Noah asked.

"My office, please," the coach looked at Noah with a blank face.

As Noah followed the coach to his office, his mind raced. He hadn't done anything wrong recently that might have gotten him into trouble. What could the coach want with him in his office? He usually only called team members to his office when they had screwed up.

When Noah entered the office, he was astonished to find his mother and sister standing near the coach's desk. But that didn't scare him. What scared him was the streaks of tears running down his mother's face and the unearthly was his sister was crying.

"Wh… what's wrong?" Noah asked as the coach closed his office door so the family can have some privacy.

"Oh, Noah… Your father had an accident… The car crashed… Tim was with him… They… They didn't make it…" the words came from his mother's mouth.

The words hit Noah like a ton of bricks. His head started spinning and he slumped to the floor, "No… no… They were just here! They watched my football game. They just left for a little while…" Noah was trying to make sense of it all.

"They hit a truck when getting on the highway. Oh, Noah…" his mother wailed.

His father… gone. His uncle… gone. Never to be seen again. Never would Noah be able to share his trauma with his father. Never would he be able to expose his uncle for the pig he really was. Never…

It seemed like an eternity. The days and weeks that followed felt like a nightmarish dream Noah couldn't wake up from. The only time he could find a little peace was when his mind was clouded with alcohol. It soothed his troubling thoughts. His family was torn apart. His mother barely came out of her room and when she did, her breath reeked of liquor. Noah could relate. He didn't blame her at all. He knew that was the way she was trying to deal with the pain.

Nicki also dealt with the pain of losing her father in her own way. Guys seemed to be her way of escaping life and its emotions. But what Noah found odd was the fact that she chose guys who were usually up to no good. These guys, are all about the street life, loved to party, and gang bang. Noah didn't want his sister to get hurt but he didn't quite have his own life together either and was unable to help Nicki dig herself out of the rut she was stuck in.

Noah had noticed Nicki come home one evening with a bruise on her lip and left eye.

When he questioned her about potentially being in an abusive relationship, she sneered, "What do you care? You do your own thing. Mom does her own thing. Dad isn't here anymore to keep us together. So let me just do my own thing and leave me alone!"

Two weeks after the incident, Nicki was found in her room where she had taken her life. Life had become too much for her. Noah wanted to be angry with her. He wanted to beg her to come back. In a way, he admired her for doing what she did. To Noah, taking one's life didn't seem like the easy way out. To him, something like that took guts; guts he didn't have.

***

Noah's mind snapped back to the present day as he finds himself standing at the grave where his father and sister are buried.

He looks at the tombstone and begins to cry. Slowly, he takes off his jersey and rests it on his sister's tombstone. He places the football the Cougars took for a win on his father's tombstone.

"We did it, Dad. This is the game ball. This is the one I caught at the back of the end zone on a fade. It was sweet," Noah looks down and wipes tears from his eyes. "I am worried about mom. She's not doing so well. She misses you. I got it though."

He then walks over to his sister's tombstone, "The cheerleaders suck without you. I miss you, sis. I love you so much."

With a final goodbye, Noah heads home to get ready for the evening's celebrations.

CHAPTER 3

Kobe Briggs is at the prison visiting his father Bo after winning the championship with the Cougars. Kobe is seated in front of the glass that separates the prisoners from the visitors.

Bo approaches wearing an orange-coloured prison jumpsuit and sits down at the glass separating them and picks up the phone, with a broad smile on his face, He has always been happy to see his son. Kobe, who has his head down and picks up the phone. Bo is excited and it's evident from the tone of his voice.

"Congratulations, son!" Bo smiled. "Me and the guys listened to the game on the radio! It was a good win and I am really proud of you, kid!"

Kobe is still looking down, "Thanks Pops, glad you were able to listen to the game all through…"

"I supported you all through the game. You need to have seen me screaming like a kid, whenever the commentator called your name!" Bo beams.

Kobe tries to suppress the sarcasm in his voice, "I love to have seen you, Dad!"

"You guys did very well this season, a well fought and deserved victory. You deserve the championship but y'all got nothing on me and my guys, we won that title too back in the day" Bo advises his son.

"Very correct Pops," Kobe still does not raise his head.

"I don't like your coach, y'all need to change him," Bo demands. "He won the championship but yet, I don't love his gameplan. Me and the boys were discussing it before I came down here."

Kobe still has his head bowed and this makes his voice not audible enough. This made Bo angry and he retorts angrily and Kobe slowly and respectfully lifts his head up.

"Look at me when I am talking to you!" Bo shouts. "I have taught you this. It's a sign of disrespect and that's one thing you were not born with. I have been teaching you this."

"I got it, Dad," Kobe mumbles.

Bo hits the glass angrily to get the attention of his son, ignoring his response. The prison officer comes close to calm Bo's temper, but Bo is not having it either with the Officer, "Would you get your filthy hands off me!"

The officer commands, "Sir, you will have to calm down, this is not the place for noise."

Bo composes himself and hisses, "I am talking to my son, and I have to right to do that however I please, do you understand me, man."

"Just try to calm down, have a seat and talk to your son. Simple as that," the officer looks at Bo with menacing eyes.

Bo is not satisfied that he made his point clear, "You don't tell me what to do and what not to do. What sort of bullshit is that, man."

Kobe pleads, "Dad, it's okay. You are causing a scene, please."

"If you explode like this again I will have to end this visit immediately," The officer says this and walks away back to the post, not waiting for a response from Bo.

Bo then calmly takes his seat and places the telephone on his ear again.

Pausing for a few moments, Kobe waits for his father to regain his breath. "I'm sorry dad, I won't do it again. Please don't make a scene again."

Bo, a little calmer now, hisses, "You just have to learn it, man. You gotta look up and be a man! And I am your dad so I deserve that respect at least, you got me."

Kobe nods his head respectfully, "Yes sir, I get you. I won't do it again but please be calm with these officers."

It looks like Bo is about to explode again, "Ignore these officers, they gotta respect me! Do they have any idea who I am? They're very disrespectful. I deserve some respect around here!"

Bo stares at the officers who ignore his daggering glares and hisses as he adjusts his chair forward, his hands still clutching the telephone.

Abruptly changing the subject, Bo asks, "So how is Mama? Is your mama okay? Hope she is staying healthy."

"Yes sir, Mama is good, she has been eating. She wasn't eating well before but she is now," Kobe lies.

"Toni is always worried and bothered about those little things that don't even make any sense. And that is when she doesn't eat. But I know she is taking care of you," Bo says.

"She is, dad," Kobe replies. "A kind woman indeed."

Bo, feeling like he still runs the family, adds, "Tell her to eat her vegetables, she is always worried about everything. This life, we only live it once, man. You gotta live it well. Tell her I will be fine. She should quit her worries."

Kobe clears his throat and tries, "I think she has the right to be worried, Dad. It's hard not to worry when you are here.

Bo's playful demeanor disappears once again, "She has the right but she shouldn't! I will be fine, at least I am not dying. It's alright here, it's not like its hell but the prison is a very free place and that is something no one will tell you as a father, I will tell you the truth. The prison is where you meet with destiny and you get to know what is really right or wrong. Who you are, and want make you go."

"I don't know about that," Kobe says in honesty. "Everyone is worried about you."

Bo laughs, "I have never been this at peace all my life and I wish I can make you experience what I am going through as a person right now."

Bo leans closer to the glass as if he wants to whisper into Kobe's ears, Kobe does same with the telephone in his hand close to his ears. Bo whispers, "Reggie?"

Kobe, knowing what his father is really asking, replies, "Yes sir...W...we see Reggie every couple weeks. He comes around the neighborhood and then leaves."

"Okay good," Bo seems more relaxed after hearing Kobe's answer. "You let me know if anything changes."

"Yes sir, I will definitely let you know," Kobe says respectfully.

There is a little silence and Kobe notices that his dad has been the one asking the question so he decides to throw his own question at his dad, "So, dad how is it like here? I hope you don't have troubles adjusting, is there any problem?"

"It's okay, here son, adjusted well enough," Bo admits. "It has been great. People think that a prison is like a cage where you are not free to do what you want to do but contrary to that. It is a place where you truly find yourself. Outside these walls, you hardly have the chance to sit and think about life but when you are within these walls you think intently about life because you have a lot of time to spare."

Kobe frowns, "Are you serious, Dad? First time I am hearing this from anyone within these walls. Doesn't it feel awkward having to stay with serial killers and murderers?"

Bo points a finger at his son, "You don't call them that son, show some respect, wouldya? They are my family in here, it's sad they just find themselves here. Learn to love people and see beyond their mistakes and errors. Everyone knows me around these walls that I never discriminate. I love everyone but if you step on my toes then I won't take it slowly with you, man. I would have to teach you a big lesson…"

Kobe speaks calmly, trying to get his father under control again, "Dad, you have to keep your cool here."

"Kobe, everyone knows me for that, I don't take shit," Bo says firmly. "I give you the way you want it. I am really tired of people trying me, I will teach you a lesson you will never forget."

"I hope you haven't fought yet, Dad. They may increase your sentence," Kobe says with concern.

"Of course, I have. Many times," Bo smiles.

"Dad, c'mon," Kobe pleads.

Bo shakes his head, ready to teach his son something about life, "Son, hear me out, would you stay quiet, when someone disrespects you? You have to stand your ground, man up or else!"

"I don't think you to beat up a guy to prove your worth," Kobe tries proving his point once again.

Bo scoffs, "So, how then should you prove it by speaking to 'em till they get bored to death..."

Bo let out a loud laugh which draws attention to himself. The officer threatens to move forward again and some of the other inmates turn their heads to look at Bo with menacing eyes.

He tries to change the subject of discussion, "What about the kids? How are they holding up on their own?"

"All good Pops..." Kobe lies again. "They miss you and want to see you."

Bo raises his voice seemingly angry and in defensive, "You know how I feel about them coming here."

"I know but..." Kobe is cut short.

"Ain't no buts...you want them to visit you in here?" Bo mutters.

"No sir," Kobe says simply.

"Just know when you get here you got family here. Jay, Kenny, Trey, Marvin...we got our own block. You will love it here. I will introduce you to the gang, my guys. We will take you around, no one can step on your toes, kid," Bo says matter-of-factly.

Kobe is silent and slowly looks down before breaking the silence, "Pops, I want to go to college. I don't want to come here. I want to have a football life, I want to stand out on the football field, you know, be different and all."

Bo laughs out mockingly and sarcastically this doesn't surprise Kobe who is playing with the telephone wire with his middle finger, "Yah me too, I also wanted to play in the NFL be the president of this damn country and fly on my private jet to Dubai to do some winter shopping... Look at me, Kobe."

Kobe slowly raises his head. He has tears streaming down his cheek, he tries to hide them but he fails. Bo is seemingly agitated at the sight.

Bo sits at the edge of the seat as he places his right hand on the glass, "I was just like you. I wanted to go to college. So did Jay, Kenny, Trey and Marvin." Bo leans forward and looks directly at Kobe. "We all did, but here we are, and it's not that bad."

"Dad, you are misunderst..." Kobe does not get the chance to finish his sentence.

Bo sits back in his chair, "I perfectly understand you. You see us as failures, right?"

"No, dad," Kobe shakes his head. "I think there's more out there for me..."

"More what?" Bo yells. "What the hell are you talking about?"

"Dad, you are misunder...." Kobe tries saving the situation.

Bo won't have any of it, "Shut your mouth, son. I know what's best for you, the earlier you realize this, the better for you to survive and move on with life. I have taken care of you since you were a kid."

"I am more than grateful for that, Dad," Kobe replies. "You taught me to play football and here I am winning the championship."

"That's right, kid," Bo agrees.

Kobe gets enough courage to say the words, "But Dad, I would go to college and play ball."

Bo slams down the phone, gets up, and walks away escorted by the prison guard. Kobe watches Bo being escorted away.

Kobe still has the phone on his hand as he watches his dad get escorted away. He is still as an officer taps him gently on his shoulder. He puts the phone down and gets up as he knows that the officer is signaling him that his time is up.

Kobe moves out to join his mother outside who obviously had refused to see his father because she feels he has done enough harm to the family already.

Toni can see that something is wrong as she watches the shadow across Kobe's face, "He hasn't learned has he?"

Kobe sighs, "Momma, it would take more than prison bars to break pops spirit. He is still set in his ways and the way he talked I knew he must have been getting into so much trouble. It will be a miracle if he doesn't rot in there."

Toni shakes her head as she makes room for Kobe in the taxi. She signals the driver to move, "Sometimes I wonder how a man could be so hard. I blame myself for the wrongs he has brought on this family. Bo is like a stench it follows us everywhere. I hope and pray you wouldn't end up like him Kobe. I hope you learn and follow a different path." She sniffs as tears gather in her eyes.

Kobe reaches out and takes his mother's hand, "Momma, I won't. I see how much pain pops has caused you. I know I have his temperament, his impatience even his looks but I'm trying momma. That's why I became a player. I want to channel my energy to positive. Pops is no role model for me. You are, Momma. You are."

Toni reaches out and kisses Kobe on the cheek, "That's my son. I raised you well Kobe. I raised you well."

Kobe nods, "But Momma, you know you would have to forgive Pops soon. You can't keep holding the hurt in. Sooner than later, you would break down under this rage you are feeling. You should come in with me next time."

Toni shakes her head from side to side, "I have thought so much about Bo, son. There are times I cry myself to sleep because of him. He hurt me and I don't know if I would be able to forgive him. He and his family have caused me a lot of ache even before you were born but I still held on to a marriage that was doomed to fail from the start just because I believed he would change. He didn't and I gave up hope but when I had you and then the others, I thought now Bo was ready to be a man. He actually said so himself. But here we are, the same old, angry, lying, murderous crook and with all the drugs, his involvement with Reggie and the gang hope had instantly become a mirage."

Kobe smiles sardonically, "Momma, I know how you feel. Pops actually said that he would love to see me behind bars like him. He said being behind bars has been good for him and he would like to see me there someday. He actually has a family in prison. He said they look out for each other."

Toni's eyes widen in terror, "No way. You will never go behind bars son. You will never experience what's like to be a thug. Son, never take what your father says to heart. He is a broken man. He doesn't know better."

"I know Momma. I know," Kobe sighs.

Kobe squeezes Toni's hand to reassure her as they ride home in silence. Kobe, however, has his own thoughts. He doesn't know what to believe or what to stand for anymore.

On one hand, he is angry that his father got himself in a position to be thrown in prison on the other hand he believes what his father says about being free in prison.

As a young African-American, he knows how freedom outside the walls of the prison isn't really freedom for us as a people. Though he has in some measure been able to gain freedom but he still feels constrained by society.

Kobe's thoughts spin around in his head. Maybe Pops is right. Maybe I need to be there with him. Whatever momma says is out of anger. She doesn't mean it. My father may seem bad but I know he isn't really bad. He is just a tough guy that has learnt how to push his way through the world by being tough.

What about my dreams of going to college? Being behind bars wouldn't help me achieve that, it would only make me a criminal just like pops. But pops said he also had a dream like that once but look where he is now. What if Pops is correct? What if my dreams of going to college are only mere wishes? What if…

Kobe voices his uncertainties only to himself and no one else. He is in doubt as to the way his life would go. All he sees is how more likely he is to spend his life behind bars than make it to college as that is the reality around him.

Kobe bites his lip as he thinks. What will be will be. There ain't nothing I can do. I will just go with the flow.

Just then his phone rings. Reggie, one of his father's drug men is calling. His heart skips a bit and he turns to see his mother sleeping. It's a long ride home.

Kobe picks up the call, "Hello Reggie!"

Reggie's voice seems excited on the other end, "Whoo! So the cub knows who's calling."

Kobe rolls his eyes, "Yeah! Pops gave me your number. Figured I could save it."

Reggie sound impressed, "How is your old man doing in there?"

"Good so far," Kobe replies.

"So he is serving his time and staying out of trouble?" Reggie asks the same question in another way.

Kobe starts to feel frustration bubbling up inside him, "Reggie, what do you want?

"Whoo!" Reggie seems pleased with Kobe's reaction. "That's a lot of fire in your voice cub. I was just checking on my man dude."

Kobe mumbles, "Well, if you wanted to see how he was doing you should go see him. Isn't that what dudes do for their dudes?"

Reggie scoffs, "Nah! Old Reggie see Bo in prison? Nah!"

"So what do you want?" Kobe asks again. "As far as I know you and my pops weren't really tight and the last time I checked y'all had beef."

Reggie laughs, "Somebody has been talking. Kobe, you really know what's up. A chip of the old block I suppose."

"Not if I have something to say about it," Kobe can no longer keep his frustration at bay. "Reggie just spill it."

"Whoo! Chill, bro," Reggie laughs. "Well, you know your pops owed me a lot of money and if Bo has been keeping you up on these matters you should know that your Pops got debts to pay."

Kobe frowns, "I don't know what you are talking about. Pops paid you everything he owed before he got busted."

Reggie replies dryly, "Was that what he told you? Bo told you he has paid his debt to me? I am genuinely shocked kiddo. If he told you that then oops! Your old man lied. He owes me loads and I have come to collect. Well, I gave you credit for being in his corner but if you are in the know then understand we got problems. Since the cops arrested your pops, we have all been laying low. Nobody wants to join Bo behind bars I tell you. But he has been there for quite a while and the police have been off our tracks so we are back in the game."

Kobe is not interested in what Reggie has to say, "That's none of my business Reggie. If you had a deal with my father it ain't any of my business. Wait till he gets out then you can collect your debt. I have nothing to do with this and I can't help you."

Reggie lets out a sly laugh, "You see, cub that's the thing. Your father made a deal that if he isn't able to pay back or whatever, you would replace him and continue to work till you have paid his debt in full. Needless to say, your pops used you as collateral."

Kobe's eyes widen as he listens to what Reggie is saying, "What? I mean what the hell?"

Toni moves in her sleep and asks with her eyes still closed, "Is everything alright, Son?"

Kobe lifts the phone from his ear, "Yes, everything is fine. Just go back to sleep."

Reggie confirms, "Dear cub, your father signed you in and if you refuse it's a pity your beautiful momma would have to pay for it with her life as well as the other kids."

Kobe, now terrified, begins to stammer, "Emm… wait… what the hell! Emm… Not fair…"

Reggie does not give Kobe much chance to reply, "Life is not always fair man. You should ask your Pops."

"What do you mean by that Reggie? Is this some kind of bullshit or what? I am not interested in your gang shit. I want to go to college," This time, Kobe is whispering so his mom doesn't hear him.

Reggie's voice turns angry, "You call this whatever? Wait till your momma's brain dances alongside your little brothers and sisters then we will know how silly this is. As for college young man, you have got to be kidding me. You have your father's shoes to fill as well as his path to take apart from the fact that no one makes it to college from the hood. Soon enough, you would be behind bars just like your father. Well, if you are in we expect to see you at Lil Joe's crib."

The line goes dead and Kobe, hysterical, calls into the phone, "Hello! Reggie! Hello!"

Toni is already wide awake and she sees how exasperated Kobe is. Kobe's hands are on his head as the car pulls over at his home.

He climbs out of the car with his mother and gives her a knowing look, "Momma whatever happens always know I love you and never planned to hurt you."

He leaves his mother as she stares at him with a confused look on her face.

Toni was born a worrier. She doesn't remember if she ever was one of those kids who climbed out of their crib, but she could bet she wasn't, because knowing herself, she would be too worried she'd fall. She worries about everything.

Now that she is smack in this so-called midlife with a husband in prison, she should know better, right? But worry still remains her albatross, although she has learned how to better deal with it.

Toni thinks that if she is lucky enough, she would eventually outgrow her worries or at least forget old worries and insert new ones to take their place. She knows worry is fruitless and groundless. Most things she worries about end up not happening, and those things she doesn't even imagine could happen will appear and sideswipe her with brute force, sending her mind spiraling.

Despite her best efforts to rid herself of her albatross, there is one worry she realizes she might never outgrow. One worry that only grows bigger with time. And that's the worry about her Kobe.

She sees and knows parents with grown children who are in constant communication with them by text—not once in a while, but more like once an hour. She sees and knows parents who don't touch base with their adult children more than about once a week. And there are some who stay in touch daily or a few times a week.

But then she wonders, does involvement translate to caring? Or does it result in adult children who don't develop the type of independence and self-esteem necessary to fight their way in the adult world that they will inevitably inherit or have already inherited? Their shoes are suddenly too big for their feet; their coping capacity strangely lacking. The preparedness factor has failed.

Yes, the world is different now, with so many ways to stay connected. But the amount of information some parents are getting from their children is threatening to make their blood pressure rise and their hearts pound with worry.

While Toni was in college, contact with her parents was relegated to the once-weekly Sunday phone call she made from a phone booth—if she remembered to gather up enough change to insert into the slots and when she ran out of coins, so did the conversation. If she was in the mood to even try. If she was lucky enough to catch her parents at home.

If she didn't reach them, she'd simply have to wait until the following week to catch up, because there was no answering machine to let them know she called, no caller ID for them to check if they missed her call, and no texting, email or any other tether to bind them together.

And they didn't file a missing person report or convince themselves she must have been kidnapped or worse. They just waited.

Had her parents had texting and social media—the ties that bind—back then, she'd suspect they would have gotten to the point where Kobe was at now. To a world of parents who worry about their adult children, after all these years.

For Toni, worrying is a way of life. It kept her mind in the present moment. It helped her to focus on what is important. Even if worrying makes her sick and takes away her ability to eat and stay healthy, she knows she needs to worry. She needs to worry about Kobe. If not, there would be no one else to worry about him. And that scared her. She needed her son to live a good life. A life that doesn't involve stepping into his father's shoes. One that doesn't involve him getting mixed up in the wrong crowd. And one where he won't be the one she had to visit behind prison bars…

CHAPTER 4

Carlos Fuentes enters the family home and is greeted by his mother, father and younger siblings. The family embraces in a hug and sits at the dinner table. They hold hands in prayer.

Santiago takes a deep breath before beginning to pray, "Father, We have gathered to share a meal in Your honor. Thank You for putting us together as a family, and thank you for this food. Bless it to our bodies Lord. We thank you for all of the gifts you've given to those around this table. Thank you for helping Carlos and his teammates use their gifts to your glory. Lord, please replace our sins and temptations with thanksgiving. Let us be people who are filled with thanks rather than sinful desires. Amen."

While the Fuentes family enjoys a family meal together, Sophia, Carlos' mom turns to him and the conversation shifts to a serious tone, "Carlos what are your plans for the future? You graduate in June."

Carlos shrugs, "Maybe college."

"What about the military?" Sophia asks, watching the expression on her son's face turn from hungry to blank.

"Not sure yet," Carlos says, not looking up from his plate of food.

"This country has done a lot for us…" Sophia lets her voice trail off to let her son think about what she had just said.

At this point, Santiago joins the conversation, "You were raised to put others before yourself. The service of the marines, soldiers, sailors and airmen does that."

Carlos sighs, "Yes Pappi."

Sophia smiles empathetically, "What about Selena? The military can provide you, Selena and your kids with a better life then we had."

Sophia turns to Santiago and continues to talk, "What few know is that there is a demonstrated tendency in this career in which it is difficult to ascend the ladder of ranks."

Santiago nods his head as Sophia speaks, all the while Carlos squirms uncomfortably in his seat.

He moves his lips as if to speak but hesitates a little, "Mama it is true that this country has done a lot for us but I have other dreams. I would like to go to college."

Santiago frowns, "How many times do I have to tell you to fight the spirit of ingratitude that rises in you Carlos? Do you even think before you speak? How ungrateful can you get?"

Sophia, sensing the tension between father and son moves to calm her husband down, "Dear, please calm down. He is still a boy, with time he will come to see reasons why he should pursue a career in the military. Do not work yourself up over this."

Carlos rolls his eyes, "Mama, I am a man now. I graduate soon. You can't keep calling me a boy. Nothing is going to change my mind."

Santiago scoffs, "Carlos you are very well still a child. You do not understand the impact your decisions will have on your future. As your parents, we know best and due to experience, we are telling you to join the army. It will secure your future."

"Pappi, you forget that this is my life, not yours," Carlos says matter-of-factly. "It's my life so I choose what to do with it. If there are any consequences, I am mature enough to handle them."

"Boy!" Santiago bellows, "You know you are confused. This minute you talk about going to Harvard and getting a degree, the next minute you talk of your interest in football. As the head of this house and your father, I have concluded that you are still very naïve so you are not in the best position to choose for yourself what you want to do. This is the reason I have decided to ensure that all your energy is channeled towards getting into the army and that's final. Please let's continue our meal in silence."

Carlos feels his anger boil over and adds sarcastically, "Silence? Of course, we wouldn't want mama's delicious food getting into the wrong channel."

Santiago stares at Carlos for a while and shakes his head. As per Santiago's instructions, the family's meal continues in silence.

Later that evening, Carlos is lying on his bed in a deep conversation with himself.

Maybe Pappi is right, Carlos thinks. If I join the army, my future is guaranteed. I can give Selena a better life. We will be very comfortable but if I go to college the probability that my life will be comfortable is not quite clear. I know I am intelligent but in life, intelligence isn't what counts. What if after College I become miserable? No! Never! I am quite driven and determined. That's the reason why I was made football captain in the first place.

Football. What about football? I am really talented in football but could I play college ball? It's also high prospect stuff. No! Pappi thinks I play football for fun and Mama will be crestfallen if I make that choice. She really isn't a fan of football and doesn't fancy her grown son running around a field chasing a ball with other grown men. Preposterous she terms it. Well, I don't really love football. I don't hate it either. I don't even know.

Carlos sits up and places his head between his palms while still in thought.

Football to me is just a thing. I do not know what to do with it but I enjoy the game. I don't know what to do. My grades… My grades are awesome and with that, I can get into Harvard. My class teacher is so confident that I will get into Harvard. I seriously want to go to Harvard. I want to get a degree. Pappi was certainly right. I am confused. This confusion is tearing me apart. There are a lot of what-ifs and uncertainties plaguing me. Should I just do what they choose for me or should I follow my heart?

What's in my heart that I want to follow? The only thing in my heart is confusion.

Carlos assumes his lying position with his arms behind his head while coming to only one conclusion as he murmurs to himself, "I am done with this shit. I will just flow with the tide."

He closes his eyes and drifts off to sleep.

***

Santiago and Sophia are sitting outside allowing the cool evening to saturate their bodies.

Santiago dreamily says, "I remember those days when I was still courting you. You were a catch and you still are. I remember how the boys in our neighborhood used to look at me with their eyes green with envy. They didn't know why such a hottie would choose a person as rough as I was."

Sophia blushes, "Oh! Santy. It was pure bliss to be in your company. You made me laugh and still make me laugh. I saw a bright future with you that is why I stuck with you. I knew you would make me so happy and our family would be such a beautiful one."

"I made mistakes," Santiago confesses. "Our life would be better than this. If Carlos stops being stubborn and joins the army our status will climb higher. Carlos will do better when he joins the army. Do you know the amount of prestige and resources that will be at his disposal? For a country that has helped us, that's the little we can give to pay back. Carlos must join the army."

"Carlos is bent on going to Harvard," Sophia tries hesitantly. "He is a really gifted child. He is multi-talented. He is very involved in football and his grades are still excellent. Not many people can manage both that. I feel we should just let him make his decision. He is mature enough to make the decision that is right for him. I trust him."

"What do you mean?" Santiago's question oozes irritation. "I thought you were on my side. Carlos is confused. He doesn't know what's good for him. Any decision he is going to make now that isn't making him join the army to me is a totally wrong decision. I really don't care about his grades. He could be an average student for all I care."

"Wait!" Sophia frowns. "I feel Carlos not being able to make a decision because he is confused is beside the point. Tell me the truth. Are you doing this for Carlos' sake or yours?"

While not looking at his wife, Santiago replies, "What do you mean? I don't understand. Carlos is my son and I want the best for him."

Sophia shakes her head in disagreement, "I don't believe you. Are you still nursing the pain of being rejected by the army? It's such a long time Santiago and I thought you had gotten over it. You told me yourself."

Santiago still evades her stare, "Sophia, you won't understand. I thought it was over but some months ago when I saw one of our neighbors' son with his badge, I felt like a knife had pierced through my heart. It was my dream to join the army but since I couldn't, Carlos my first son will live that dream. Carlos will live my dream and he won't regret it."

Sophia sits quietly for a moment while reveling in disbelief, "Unbelievable! All this time I thought you were concerned for Carlos. No! Santiago this is selfish. That boy is an excellent student and athlete. He has a lot of potential. Though we are grateful to this country for helping us start over, it's no criteria for pushing our son into what he has no interest in. Carlos can serve this country via other means using his gifts. You shouldn't force him to join the army. You will regret it if you do Santiago."

Santiago feels his anger boil over, "Woman! You dare question me. You challenge me, Sophia. I love you, I love my son that's the reason I have made this decision for him. He will join the army and that's final."

Sophia spits back, "Jeez! Santiago, when did you become so conceited? A good father only guides his children. You have trained Carlos well and you should trust that he will make the right decision. It's his life after all."

Santiago does not see his wife's reason, "A child is a child no matter how grown he or she is. Santiago is still a child and as such I must help him choose. The boy is a walking confusion. He doesn't know what to do. I can't trust him with such sensitive decision. Like I said earlier, this decision is final. Nobody can change my mind. Nobody, not even you."

With that, he stands and walks away.

Sophia begs, on the verge of tears, "Santiago! Don't do this, please. Let Carlos make his decision himself. I beg you."

***

Carlos, who wakes up from the elevated voices of his parents, picks up the phone to call his girlfriend.

When she answers, Carlos tells her about his conversation with his father earlier in the evening, "I have tried convincing them but it seems their minds are made up. They act like I am still a child. It's not fair babe. I feel like a stranger to my parents, especially my dad. I have told him countless times already that I don't want to join the army but the guy thinks I am too confused to make a real decision. I am tired."

While Carlos is explaining the situation to Selena, his mother enters the room.

Carlos stops talking for a moment and then says into the phone, "I will call you back babe. I love you."

Sophia smiles at her son, "Carlos dear, was that Selena?"

Carlos sighs, "Yes mama."

"I knew it the moment I saw your face a second ago," Sophia says. "She has this effect on you. You glow. Just the way your father makes me glow."

"I love her mama," Carlos confesses. "She loves me too and trusts that any decision I make will be the best for both of us. But you and Papa have refused to see reasons with me. I am not a child anymore. Why can't you see that?"

"I trust you son. I do. It's just that your father…" Sophia lets her voice trail off.

Carlos scoffs, "He doesn't trust me enough. Sometimes I wonder if he really wants me to join the army because it's the best prospect for me though I disagree with him or he is pushing me to join the army because he wants to live his dream through me."

Sophia, not wanting to admit that Carlos is speaking the truth, decides to reason with her son once more, "Your Papa loves you, Carlos. That's all you should know and understand. Your father wants an answer a few days from now. You should have decided by then."

Carlos sighs, "Mama, in a few days I will be giving a valedictory speech at school. I really do not have time to argue with Papa because my mind is unchanged. I am going to Harvard. For my football talent, I will join the football club there. I will pursue my dreams alongside develop my talent. Tell Papa my mind is unchanged. Joining the army is not an option for me."

"Carlos, I understand your decision. But for one listen to your father. He may be right," Sophia says.

"I can't place my life on the fact that Papa may be right. May being the operative word. If I am taking a risk, I want to take a risk based on what I know I want," Carlos admits.

Sophia sighs, "I am tired of arguing with you both. I am just tired. How can father and son be at loggerheads over a matter that can be settled amicably?"

"Papa is hell-bent on his decision and I am hell-bent on mine," Carlos states.

Sophia changes the subject, "Have you written out your valedictory speech yet?"

"Not yet, but I will," Carlos replies, happy to talk about something else.

Sophia looks at her son, "I trust you."

Carlos takes a deep breath, "I wish Papa felt that way too."

"He does. He is just…" Sophia let the conversation come to an end. She knows there is nothing left to say that hasn't already been said at least ten times before.

When Carlos settles down for a few hours of restless sleep before dawn, he finds himself in a somewhat disturbing dream.

He finds himself sitting with his parents in the living room.

His father has a satisfied expression on his face and says, "Carlos I am super happy for you. In fact, I can't tell you how elated I feel. I am a proud to be your father."

Carlos sits, still not saying a word.

Sophia seems agitated, "Carlos dear, are you fine? You look pale."

"Sure Mama," Carlos says. "Everyone is happy now."

"Are you really happy?" Sophia asks.

"Does it matter?" Carlos replies. "Papa is proud of me. That's enough motivation."

Sophia grips Carlos' shoulders and squeezes them, "Everything will be fine."

Santiago smiles, "Everything is sure fine. In fact, everything will be better once you get to the camp. When you see your mates serving their country with so much enthusiasm, you will be inspired. As it is now, one of the Fuentes is in the army.”

The scene in front of Carlos changes and in his dream, he finds himself in his own room, on the verge of tears. As he notices his mother entering the room, he quickly wipes away the tears before he faces her.

Sophia sighs, “Oh! My boy. I am so sorry. I know how you must feel.”

Carlos breaks down as he faces her, “Mama, I got into Harvard. I actually got into Harvard. I held the acceptance letter in my hands. Mama, I had my dreams in my hands until Papa threatened to disown me. Mama!”

Sophia embraces him while soothing him with her hand on his back, “My boy, I am so sorry. I am really sorry. I couldn’t help you. I watched as your father tore your dreams out of your hands. I thought you were too young to understand but now I understand that you have grown up to be a man who is sure of the path that he wants his path to take. I should have fought harder. I am sorry.”

Carlos replies amidst tears, “I am tired of fighting. All my dreams have been washed down the drain because of Papa’s selfishness. This painful and it hurts so bad.”

Sophia murmurs, “I know. There’s nothing we can do now. You just have to put yourself together and move on. You are a smart young man. You will find a way.”

Again, the scene in front of Carlos starts to fade and in his dream, he now sees his mother moving towards the front door, ready to open it when he hears a knock.

Santiago frowns, "We aren't expecting anybody, are we?"

"None, dear," Sophia says as she opens the door and sees a postman outside.

She exchanges pleasantries with the postman and collects the parcel from him.

As she closes the door behind her, she says, "We have a parcel. It should be from Carlos."

Santiago doesn't pay too much attention and asks, "What's in the parcel?"

Sophia opens the parcel and sees a badge alongside a letter, "There's a badge with Carlos' name on it. And a letter."

"What does the letter say?" Santiago asks.

"What is his badge doing here while he is still in camp?" a frown crosses Sophia's face.

"Well, open it," Santiago demands.

Sophia opens the letter and reads, "No! No! No! This can't be. No!" She shakes and lowers herself to the ground.

Santiago, now clearly concerned, rushes to her side, "What is the matter? What did the letter say?"

Sophia, crying, hands over the letter to Santiago and he too reads through it, "This boy has disgraced us. How dare he?"

Sophia, her face streaked with tears, wails, "My poor boy. Where is he now? I want him to come home. I won't force him back. Carlos baby just come back home."

Santiago is irritated and snaps at his wife, "Stop that, woman! Stop that! I blame you for pampering this boy. It's your fault this shame is upon us. He acted like a coward. It would have been better that he didn't go than for him to go and escape two weeks later. This is purely shameful. I will be a laughing stock by the time…"

Sophia slowly stands to her feet and faces her husband, "Oh! Stop. It's not always about you. Can you just pause a moment and analyze your actions these few months. You pressured this boy. You pressured him even when he told you to your face he didn't want to join the army. Now my baby has escaped to God knows where."

Santiago fumes, "Come off it. He isn't a baby anymore. He is a full-grown man."

"Oh! He's a grown man to you now," Sophia spits. "Didn't you imply earlier that he was too young to decide what to do with his life? You are contradicting yourself now and it shocks me."

Santiago, exasperated, runs his hand over his face in a gesture of worry, "Where could he be? Where would he have gone?"

Sophia pushes past him and says, "I am going to call Selena. He may have reached her…"

Carlos' eyes snap open as he gasps for air. A small glimpse of sunlight peers through his bedroom curtain as he realizes he had just awoken from a nightmare, a nightmare he wishes won't come true…

CHAPTER 5

Dre Banks opens the door to find his family in the living room in front of the television. His younger brother and sister run to hug him as soon as he enters the house as his parents stand up clapping. He walks into the living room and his mother walks over and hugs him then finally Otis, his father.

They engage in a long hug as Otis says, "Proud of you son...scouts from every division one college were there. You can play anywhere you want."

Dre sighs, "Anywhere I want...really? At quarterback?"

"C'mon Dre not now, not this..." Otis frowns.

"If they want me to play receiver?" Dre asks. "Running back? Be a DB? Not interested...I am a quarterback!"

"You have to consider your future," Otis presses on. "Your best shot to make it to prime time ain't at quarterback. You know how this system works."

Dre is emotional, angry, animated and raises his arms and voice. He starts counting with his fingers as he mentions players' names, "It's not like that anymore! Russell Wilson, Patrick Mahomes, Lamar Jackson, Jalen Hurts, Deshaun Watson, Kyler Murray, Jameis Winston, Justin Fields, Jacoby Brissett..."

"Dre," Otis interrupts, "Let me tell you about Chuck Ealey. Like you, he was 53-0 as a quarterback. Undefeated. Untouched."

Otis steps closer to Dre seemingly begging to get his point across, "His 35-0 at Toledo is the NCAA record yet no National Football League club was willing to give him a chance at quarterback. He had to go to Canada to play quarterback."

"Dad, I know about the gentleman's agreement in 1933 by NFL owners not to hire black players," Dre starts counting with his fingers as he says the names. "I know about Warren Moon, Jimmy Jones, Condredge Holloway, Damon Allen, Tracy Ham, Danny Barrett, Kevin Glenn Henry Burris, Roy Dewalt, Bernie Cutis. I know them all, Dad. I respect them all. I know what they did, but it's not like that anymore."

"Do you know Colin Kapernick?" Otis asks.

"C'mon, Dad," Dre tries again. To him, engaging in conversation with his father over football always seems to bring out the worst in both of them.

"He's unemployed," Otis states without flinching.

"But..." Otis tries once more.

Otis cuts him off, "But what Dre? He graduated from college with a 4.0 and got 37 on the Wonderlic! You know what the Wonderlic is... right?"

"Yeah, the intellect test the NFL gives," Dre confirms.

"That's right," Otis nods his head. "He's smart and athletic like you. But he's unemployed Dre because he was protesting the oppression of black people and people of color. This system ain't for us."

Dre turns his head and points to the couch, "Dad, I get it. We sat right there watching Jay z in a Kap jersey rap the lyric, Once I said no to the Super Bowl. You need me, I don't need you..." He turns back and looks at Otis, "Every night we in the end zone. Tell the NFL we in stadiums too."

"So why did he chose to collaborate with the NFL?" Otis asks.

"Like Jay said, I'm not a businessman. I'm a business, man," Dre acknowledges.

"Well, that business, has given the NFL guilt-free access to black audiences, culture, entertainers and influencers," Otis takes a step back seemingly feeling distraught. "You can't question Jay-Z's commitment to social justice. He has consistently used his platform to have critical conversations and bring awareness to the inequalities and injustices that black people regularly face."

Otis pats his left-hand palm with the back of his right hand, "He executive produced a riveting six-part documentary series on the slain teen Trayvon Martin."

They are both silent looking at each other.

Dre sighs, "You know what Dad? The problem is not with the system at least not anymore. The problem is that you do not believe in me and that hurts more than the stack of odds piled against me."

Otis runs his hand down his face, "No son, it's not that I don't believe in you. I am a father and what fathers do best is to protect their kids."

Dre feels exasperated, "Protect their kids? Of course, fathers protect their kids from threats not from living their dreams. Dad, we always go in circles with this thing. You have your ideology of what you want for me but I have mine and as it stands, if I am going to keep playing, I will stick to being a quarterback."

"Back in the days," Otis rolls his eyes, "Children weren't as stubborn as they are now. I wonder what is happening to this generation."

"We have simply chosen to live on our own terms, Dad," Dre challenges his father.

Just then, Cheryl enters with a tray of food and places it on the table, "Come on guys, food is ready."

Dre walks over to the table, "Smells nice, Mum. My mouth is watery already. What do we have here?" He picks up a plate and serves himself generously.

Otis, who was quiet for a few seconds, creases his forehead in anger, "If you would just listen…"

Cheryl quickly diffuses the heat that is about to rise, "Not now dear. Not now. Let's just enjoy this meal and be grateful for the win Dre had today."

Dre smiles with gratitude in his eyes, "Thank you, Momma."

Cheryl nods and smiles at Dre as they eat their meal in silence.

After the meal, Dre goes outside to shoot some hoops in order to avoid his father.

While watching her son disappear on the other side of the kitchen door, Cheryl looks over to Otis, "Have you heard of the word trust?"

Otis, sensing where the conversation is heading, is defensive, "You won't understand these things. I am his father and you and I know how blacks are the least in the chain and being a black quarter black portends more failure for Dre who is a promising young man. He thinks he is as equal as the white dudes but that's just delusional. I can begin to count how many black quarterbacks are unsuccessful. Many had their profession frustrated by the system."

"I won't say I don't understand the point you are coming from but there are still a handful of blacks who have built a successful career by being quarterbacks. Dre plays better as a quarterback and you know it," Cheryl points out.

"A handful, you say," Otis remarks. "My son can't take such a risk while I am still alive. I am here to protect him. A hand full of successful black quarterbacks is not solid enough for him. If he must be a quarterback then the system must be totally revamped which we know won't be as quick as we will wish for it too. It may take years and Dre Banks doesn't have ten years."

"What happened to only fools see the futility of their dreams and rest on their oars?" Cheryl asks. "That was what you used to tell Dre when he was younger. Now…"

Otis raises his hands in desperation, "That was such a long time ago, Cheryl. Dre was still a kid and not a young man faced with slim choices. This is real life Cheryl and in real life, shit happens. I want to protect my son from that shit. No matter how I explain it to you, you won't get it."

Cheryl looks at her husband, clearly offended, "Can you imagine? Otis, this is unbelievable. You just insinuated that because I am totally clueless about how life works. I feel insulted Otis. If there's anyone to understand it's me. It's me, Otis. I carried that boy in my womb for nine solid months. I felt the pain. I brought him out. From his baby years, I have watched him grow into this wonderful, promising young man. I know the dreams he carries on his shoulders, dreams you are making heavier for him with your insensitive expectations. I see how hard he works at being the best at everything. Dre is a gifted child and most times you don't see it. The only thing you see is how to change who he is. You crush his spirit anytime you dismiss his wins. From his academic wins even to his wins in sports. You are not comfortable with the fact that Dre has learned to be at home in his beautiful black skin and you have not. Dre has accepted who he is and the gifts he has. Whether you like it or not, Dre is a wonderful black quarterback who will be successful at whatever he chooses no matter how solid your doubts are. You may wish to change the gifts he has but you can never change who Dre is at heart. The sooner you realize this, the better for you."

Cheryl stomps out angrily. There is no way she is going to engage in another fruitless fight she knows she would not be able to win. Otis stares after her in shock.

After a few seconds, he mutters to himself, "Whoooo! Cheryl came on so strong. Where is all the anger coming from? I just want the best for my son. Is that so wrong? Nobody understands me. Son and mother have taken sides against me. If Dre could change his field of play. He would make a successful DB or even receiver. Anything but a quarterback."

***

"Dre, can we go out for a walk?" Cheryl asks as she walks over to where her son is getting ready to shoot a ball into a basketball net hanging from the entrance of the garage.

"Sure, Momma. I am taking it all in… You know how it goes…," Dre drops the ball and follows his mother.

Cheryl places her hand across Dre' shoulders, "You look a little better, Son. It helps if you just let it go and concentrate on something that you are good at."

Dre smiles, "Yeah! I guess. That's what happens when I eat your food. You are a wonderful cook, Momma. I know one day I will get someone just as wonderful as you."

Cheryl laughs, "What about that girl that came to see you the other day? Isn't she wonderful?"

Dre chuckles, "No, Momma, she is just a friend."

Cheryl winks at her son, "Just a friend? She is really beautiful, you know."

Dre continues, "Momma, she is just a friend and nothing more. Besides, there's more to a person that what she looks like. I for one won't settle for a lady just because of the way she looks."

Cheryl nods in agreement, "That's so smart. Really smart. Anytime I look at you, I know I did the right thing. You are real gentleman Double A."

Dre's eyes grow wide, "Momma! Who taught you to call me by that name?"

Cheryl shrugs, "I heard your friends talking to you the other day and they called you Double A."

"Momma! You were listening in on our conversation. That's not so cool," Dre shook his head.

"Oh!" Cheryl presses on, "Because I call you a Double A now makes me not cool. That's not nice, Son."

Dre laughs, knowing what his mother is thinking, "No, Momma. They call me Double A in mockery. It means All American. They call me that because I am excellent at sports and academics. I am the ideal American son. About being cool, Momma you are so cool and you will always be cool to me. You are way cooler than Dad, I must say."

Cheryl seizes the opportunity, "Dre, your father is a good man and you know it. He is just scared for you. With the system, a father should be scared. He is really concerned for you.

"Momma, I understand the part of him being scared for me but what I don't get is his forcefulness," Dre confesses. "Since I was a child, I really never made any choice of my own. Dad had been the one who made my decisions for me. I didn't see it as a problem then but now, it's really getting to me. I am almost a grown man now. I am in senior year for crying out loud. As far as I know, I have been a good son. Some say the best any father could wish for me. I have done all Dad wanted me to but I am grown now and this is the perfect time to start making serious decisions for myself. I am no longer tied to Dad's apron strings. This is what he doesn't understand. He feels I am still a child."

"Dre!" Cheryl scolds. "Come on. You should know your dad by now. He expresses his care and love by worrying over you. You should know by now and you should understand that he wants the best for you. It is true that the NFL hasn't always been kind to black quarterbacks. His worry and fear for your future are not baseless or unfounded. This is a reality that we know you will face."

"Momma," Dre sighs, "I have thought this through. For some time, I contemplated changing my field of play but I couldn't. You know I am a quarterback. So, I don't want to try to fit into a mold that is obviously not meant for me. It's totally foolhardy to try to fit a square peg in a round hole. If I stop playing as a quarterback, it's me trying to fit into a mold that isn't me and that will be frustrating. More people have died from frustration and depression than from any other thing. Momma, you should understand me better."

"Oh! My baby, I understand you," Cheryl says caringly. "I understand perfectly. But I want you to see through your father's lenses too. You both really need to put an end to your bickering. I don't like the energy you both have towards each other."

"Momma, you should talk to him," Dre suggests. "He should let me be. I will be fine."

Cheryl runs her hand over Dre's face, "I know you will, Son. I am sure you will."

As Dre and his mother enter their house again, Otis looks up from the football game he is watching on television.

"Come, sit with me," Otis says and Dre follows.

"Oh!" Dre smiles "You are watching a match. I know the Dogs will win."

"I don't think so, Son," Otis laughs. "The Tigers have the best defense. Their game plan is always on point."

Dre shakes his head in disagreement, "No, Dad. The quarterback sucks. He can't throw and that's going to be a big problem. See, the other quarterback can read defenses and can make something out of nothing."

Otis points at a player on the screen, "That dude is a white quarterback. In fact, the quarterbacks of the two teams are both whites. What does that tell you, Son?"

Dre senses where the discussion is heading once more and quickly stands to exit, "No, Dad. We are not doing this again. Not right now. I do not have the mental energy to withstand any argument with you. Not now, not ever."

Dre turns to work out.

Otis raises his voice, "You know that's disrespectful, Dre. You know what you are about to do is wrong. As your father, I know what's best for you. I know the path you should take because I have been around for a long time. I will not have you disrespect me. Not now, not ever."

Dre stops in his tracks, "What? What's best for me? Did you just say what's best for me? That's like the biggest joke of the century. Dad, can you remember when I was to represent my school in a science competition? How I was so excited about it? Do you remember how I felt when you shut me down and told my teacher that I only wanted to be involved in sports competitions even though you knew how badly I wanted to represent my school? Can you remember how miserable I felt and how I cried myself to sleep throughout that month? Dad, back then you didn't know what was best for me and now you are still so clueless."

Otis looks at his son, his eyes wide with anger, "How dare you? After all..."

Dre cuts him short, "After all, you have done for me? Come on, Dad. What you have done for me are the basic responsibilities of a father. There's nothing special about dad that. If you had been there for me emotionally then you would have earned the right to say those words."

Otis shakes with anger, "How dare you? Dre Banks, how dare you? I have invested so much in you because I want you to be better than me. Everything I did, I did out of love but you stand here to throw everything in my face? What the hell!"

"Dad!" Dre shouts, equally angry, "I should say I am sorry because that's the right thing to do but I won't. I have been a walking volcano ready to erupt at any moment. They say I am the perfect son and that you did a good job of raising me. But today, I choose to be imperfect because that perfect mold isn't mine. I am a flawed kid dad. You have to see it for what it is and just to add. I am going to NFL to play as a quarterback and that's not because I want to run it in your face but because this is my life and I want to live it on my own terms."

He turns and makes his way to the bedroom while his father watches, utterly bewildered.

Cheryl enters and she observes the tense atmosphere, "What's wrong now?"

"That boy is no son of mine," Otis yells and looks back to the television screen.

***

That evening, Cheryl sits with her mobile phone in her hand, looking at an article that was written about that day's game on the school's digital newspaper.

A picture of her son stares back at her, "Oh! My boy is a star. A big star."

"What's with the excitement?" Otis asks as he looks over her shoulder at the article on her phone.

"Dre has been featured in the school newspaper as a fast-growing talent. Here, see," Cheryl says as she hands the phone to him.

Otis seizes it as his eyes shine with unintended curiosity, quickly reading through it, "That's my boy. I knew he was meant for big things. I knew he would make an amazing quarterback. I am super happy for him."

Cheryl looks at him in surprise, "You? Really! Have you forgotten about the fight you had earlier today? "Are you being patronizing now?"

Otis smiles weakly, "I know Cheryl. I know now. I was wrong. It was pride. You need to forgive me."

Cheryl shakes her head, "It is Dre you need to talk to, not me."

Otis shrugs, "I have tried talking to him before he went to bed but it seems like he is still angry with me."

"His anger is justifiable," Cheryl admits. " He has every right to be angry with you. You were angry because he had the guts to tell you to your face that you are a controlling father. Something you couldn't take but it's true. Otis, it's true. You are a controlling man. Maybe you don't see it but we do. All of us in this house have shivered under you for so long. Otis, at the time I didn't know what to say to you. But now, now you stand here and talk like you have been his support system from the word go. That, I can't take."

Otis runs his hand down his face, "Cheryl I know I messed up big time. It was fear. I allowed fear to control me. I allowed fear to be my driving force. About being controlling Cheryl, you knew I was like this yet you married me."

Cheryl sighs, "I am sorry. The words didn't come out the way I wanted them to. I am mad at you. Since your fight with Dre earlier today I doubted if you were the same man I fell in love with. I didn't know how to get it out and it just came out unexpectedly. But despite your imperfections, I know you are a good man. I know you are a good father. I have watched you sacrifice your life for our kids. You do a great job being a great father but you need balance."

Otis smiles apologetically, "That's why I need you. You have been the balance in my life. Without you, my world would have been upside down. I can do the things I do because you are in my life. I know I was wrong but at that moment, I was talking from a depth of negative emotions. I wanted to take my words back but I couldn't. You know me and my stubbornness. Cheryl, I have hurt you and my son. I won't deny that but what I won't take is you holding the hurt against me. We shouldn't be like this Cheryl."

Cheryl breaks down in tears, "Otis, you hurt me and my son. I begged you but you wouldn't listen. You just wouldn't let my boy be. I was angry but now after seeing how well my boy is doing, I forgive you. Dre was angry but not anymore. I spoke with him before he fell asleep this evening."

With that, Cheryl nods her head in the direction of Dre's room.

Otis smiles and within a few seconds, he is standing in front of his son's closed bedroom door. He knocks gently and opens the door.

Dre, still wide awake, sees his father and sits up in bed, "Momma said she would talk to you…"

Otis sits down next to his son on the bed, "Son. You have made me a really proud father. I am here brimming with pride. After all, I did to you I shouldn't…"

Dre sighs, "Come on, Dad. There's no need. I should be the one apologizing. That was no way to talk to a father and a good one at that. I appreciate you looking out for me and I am really sorry for being insensitive."

Otis smiles uncomfortably, "It took your mother effort to make me realize that I was too hard on you. Forgive me."

"Come on, Dad," Dre nods. "We are good. You should come to watch my next game. I have booked a ticket for you."

Otis got up and walked out, happy to know he has mended things with his son.

Dre, on the other hand, still sits on his bed in the dark with his headphones and music blasting, knowing it would only be a matter of time before his father forgets that he has even apologized. Then they would be back to square one…

CHAPTER 6

Noah comes home to find his mother passed out in her bedroom with an empty bottle of booze in her hand. He takes the bottle out of his her hand and places it on the side table then covers her with a blanket.

"You are an alcoholic," he whispers, then goes into her bathroom and takes a bottle of alcohol out of the cabinet. Without hesitation, he takes a swig, heads back and kisses her on the forehead.

As he watches his mom sleep, he thinks back to a woman who had visited the school during assembly a few weeks ago. She had prepared a speech and stood nervously in front of Noah, his friends, the entire school and a handful of teachers.

"My mother was an alcoholic," she began. "I knew this from the time I was about eight years old, without anyone ever telling me. In fact, we avoided talking about it. And one thing my increasingly drunk mother did really early on was stop showing up. At first, I thought she had just forgotten me. Which, on the one hand, she had. But on the other, she was drunk, which I know now means that the forgetting was a symptom, not the reason: She forgot because she was drunk, not because she disliked me."

"This dissonance — that my sober mother loved me very much, that she braided my hair and sang to me, bought me little matching jumpers and sock sets, and made sure I was inoculated and had a lunch packed with little love notes in pen on the napkin tucked inside, but then forgot to even bother picking me up occasionally, with barely a nod in my direction in apology after the fact — this dissonance that I began to experience, where suddenly I wasn't first on her list but now seemed last, was quite confusing. I was too confused to take it personally. I felt nervous, and it was the nervousness that I would also keep for years to come."

"Mostly, my mother drank when I was in bed and my father was working late or wasn't home. So I didn't actually experience my drunk mother right off the bat too much. I would experience the very beginning of it, at the end of the school day, when she was just getting rolling, or I would experience the tail end of it, when she seemed groggy or out of sorts the next morning. Those times I woke up and the usual morning routine was absent; no one was making breakfast. Sometimes, I learned, there were no lunches packed for school."

"In the night, I would get up to go to the bathroom or get a drink of water, and though it seemed very late, instead of the house being quiet, there were the unmistakable sounds of life: creaking floorboards, a closing cupboard. My mother would be down the hall, in the kitchen, on the phone. Hearing one side of a conversation is so odd to begin with; it's like eavesdropping, but the picture painted seems much more mysterious than if you could hear the other person. It had to be after 10:00, 11:00 at night. Who was she talking to?"

""'You're an alcoholic," I said to her, not yet nine years old, a little kid in pigtails. I didn't judge. I crawled beside her and hugged her."

"As an adult, I would have one strategy for dealing with my mother: No matter what, under no circumstances would I answer the phone after 5 p.m. Any breaking of this rule always resulted in a horrible conversation that I regretted and she forgot. My husband's father always said, "Nothing good happens after 1 a.m." Well, with my mother that was true, except it was 5 p.m. You could hear in her voice the moment she started drinking, and in fact, in later years, I sometimes took a call at a safe time — say 4:30 p.m., right when she was leaving work, only to have the call drift into an unsafe, post–5:00 p.m. drinking time. I'd hear the beer can crack open, and within a few minutes her voice thickened and slowed. Within a half-hour she was argumentative or, worse, sad."

"A full-on encounter with my drunk mother late at night was something I instinctively avoided. As a child, I was not yet a worthy adversary or sounding board for her. In fact, from about the age of eight to 13, when my mother drank, I became invisible. I had to graduate to teenager in order to be interesting to her. In some ways, when I think back on it, though my teenage years were more explosive and harder, the childhood ones were so much lonelier, quieter, and sadder. So much more desolate."

"I knew that my mother was an alcoholic before I knew the word for it, and I guarded this knowledge as if it were my own secret, not hers. I was, as a sober person, even at the age of eight, better at hiding her alcoholism than she was, anyway. And she was pretty good for a while. This threw off the mother-child dynamic considerably, and I grew up to be a textbook adult child of an alcoholic. But we learned what alcoholism was at school, probably in third grade. This fact, the naming of the problem, worried me because it sounded very serious, but it also simplified my focus. And it was like the last piece in a jigsaw puzzle for me: This made sense. I felt relief as I worked this out, the fact that her personality changed sometimes, that she became less reliable. All of it made sense and helped me to organize my feelings around alcoholism as a disease rather than simply something to hide and be embarrassed about."

"Alcoholism teaches you to compartmentalize your relationships, and even though I was very young, I did this quickly. I didn't talk to my brothers about it very much. I didn't ask my father many questions. There were no group discussions. Ironically, the only person I could be fully honest with in this situation was my mother."

"I think about those early confrontations with my mother now and I cringe, the idea of a small child coming to her and saying, "Here, I found the answer. I know what is wrong with you, and there is a solution." I felt, once I'd latched onto the concept of alcoholism, a great relief: Here was a plan, with a fix. Just like me later as an adult, I spent a long time paralyzed by inertia and fear and anxiety, and then I latched onto a solution that spurred me to action. The path seemed clear. I only needed to confront my mother carefully and present her with my plan."

"What I didn't know yet was how poorly that would go and how poorly it would always go. For all the lying by omission I learned to do for the outside world, my mother and her alcoholism honed techniques for evasion and lying that I simply would never be able to breach. I was at the beginning, not the end, of trying to mobilize and change her. And though I would feel nothing but defeat over and over, I still know today that it was better than to live with not trying."

"I told her that there was even a cure for this! There was help for it; it was simple. "You're an alcoholic," I said to her, not yet nine years old, a little kid in pigtails. I didn't judge. I crawled beside her and hugged her. She assured me that she was fine, she reassured me that I was safe, that she loved me. And she ignored me."

"My mother hid her drinking from my father but not from me. She either considered me too stupid or knew that I would never tell on her."

"Adult Children of Alcoholics, much like Al-Anon, describes the way that being parented by or loved by an alcoholic changes you. Most commonly, and what I found to be most true for myself, was the fact that I lost my own identity. I was always nervous; I dreaded and handled personal criticism very poorly; and more than anything else, I found it easier to focus on other people than to focus on myself. This part, what I think of as "the killer," is something I struggle with today: I can always find someone else to focus on rather than take care of myself or my own business. I was, in some ways, erased."

"But before I became an adult child of an alcoholic, I was first and foremost the child of one. The only daughter of an alcoholic mother of four. I knew with most of my being what was wrong with her from about the third grade and was certain of it by the fifth. By then, I would have walked through a fire for her, and there was occasionally the sense that such a scenario might actually be necessary. This — the child willing to walk through the fire for the parent — is a classic hallmark of kids with alcoholic parents. Flipped roles, confused emotional responses: Nearly all my feelings for my mother then and even many of them now can be explained by an entry-level rehab counselor as "part of this shit.""""

"I think I probably knew that my mother drank too much, too often, even years before my father did, but I wasn't going to let him know it. I have always believed this because my mother eventually stopped drinking around my father at all; she hid her drinking from him but not from me. She either considered me too stupid or knew that I would never tell on her. This is one of the most upsetting and manipulative parts of a relationship with an alcoholic parent: They use you and turn you, inadvertently, into their protector, a liar. I became secretive and guarded, not just around friends but even around my own immediate family. I could have resisted; I could have raised hell and told my father every time that she drank, but I just wanted peace and hoped that each time was the last."

"All I wanted was for it to stop, for her to simply cease being what she was. I didn't have a concept of alcoholism as a disease, and with a child's sad and frightening simplicity, I figured that she simply could stop if she wanted to. She probably could stop for me. Why would someone do something that they knew was bad for them, that made them different than their ideal self? Only a child would oversimplify this; only a child could see reality so clearly, as this is, honestly, the problem every alcoholic must face eventually: The only solution is the simplest, hardest thing in the world. Stop."

"I knew this so well and so fast and so completely. And yet I was so powerless. Little did I know how long I would remain powerless and how it would tear me apart, ruining relationships and holidays and life events, overshadowing, degrading. It added nothing, only taking away."

"Years later, I look back at my attempts to reach out to my mother and my attempts to make friends, and I see that they were all in the shadows of my growing sense of my mother's disease. Her disease crippled my ability, even into adulthood, to be honest and open enough with people to make true connections."

"But having my daughter, Zelda, changed all of that. I know that I have Zelda to thank for my midlife burst of social activity. She, through sheer force of her existence but also through her sunny and able way, showed me that sometimes it's best to get to know people. Sometimes, it's best to reach out and share things. Sometimes, it's best to simply burst into tears when you're having a bad day. It's okay to cry in public. It's okay to tell someone you're in pain. I'd spent much of my childhood trying to be an adult. Now I get to spend a small piece of my adulthood occasionally being exactly like a baby, my emotions sometimes overwhelming me, calling out to strangers and old friends. Helping random people on the street who'd dropped everything out of their purse or who simply looked lost. Zelda changed the way that I interacted with everyone."

"I learned, well into adulthood, that changing my mother was never an option, no matter how I struggled. But that didn't mean that change wasn't possible. It was simply that the changes would be in me…"

Noah's thoughts are snapped back to reality as he hears his mother's footsteps shuffling towards the bathroom. Instantly, Noah's legs begin to move and within seconds, he is met with his mother hanging her head over the toilet seat.

By now, he has become used to the odd noises she makes when she throws up.

His mother looks up at him apologetically for a few seconds and then tilts her head back over the toilet seat.

"I don't judge you…" Noah whispers, although he knows his mother won't even remember he has just said that.

To Noah, her drinking is not something he hates. Yes, he doesn't like the fact that she is groggy or sick half the time. He really doesn't like the way her personality has deteriorated. But in a strange way, he felt that she needed to drink. The drinking made her forget. It made her feel a buzz Noah had also become fond of.

As his mother stands up from the bathroom floor, splashes a little water on her face and goes back to her bedroom without looking at her son, Noah knows that he cannot sit between these walls for another night.

Once he sees his mother securely in bed again, he glances at a framed image of his father and his sister.

"You are not allowed to judge either, you know that, don't you?" Noah talks to the faces in the photograph.

"And you…" Noah points to the picture of his deceased sister, "You… Do you know that it can be hard to think about suicide, much less talk about it. Many people shy away from the subject, finding it frightening, even impossible to understand. And suicide certainly can be hard to understand, since it's not always clear why a person makes this choice."

When Noah doesn't get a response from his sister in the imaginary conversation he is having with her, he continues, "It's not always possible to tell if someone's considering suicide. Experts agree that a number of warning signs can suggest a person might have suicide on their mind, but not everyone shows these signs. It's also important to keep in mind that simply thinking about suicide doesn't automatically lead to an attempt. What's more, these "warning signs" don't always mean that someone's contemplating suicide. That being said, if you know someone who shows any of the following signs, it's best to encourage them to talk to a therapist or other healthcare professional as soon as possible. But in general, suicide often isn't just an impulsive act. To people who consider it, it might seem like the most logical solution."

Noah turns away from the picture, fetches a bottle of booze from the kitchen and takes another swig. While holding it in his hand, he walks over to his sister's photograph again and continues his conversation, "Some people might view talking about suicide as nothing more than a plea for attention. But people considering suicide have often thought about it for some time. These thoughts come from a place of deep pain and it's essential to take their feelings seriously. Others might feel that suicide is a selfish act. And it's understandable to feel this way, especially if you've lost a loved one to suicide. How could they do this, knowing the pain it would cause you? But this notion is false, and it does a disservice to people considering suicide by minimizing their pain. This pain can eventually become so difficult to cope with that contemplating even one more day seems unbearable."

Noah laughs, "But I am sure you already know all this… You are the expert, after all…"

For a few minutes, Noah stands, staring at the pictures. Then he turns his back and walks out of the house.

CHAPTER 7

Santiago is sitting on the couch in the living room, deep in thought, "It's been an hour now and that son of mine hasn't shown. He doesn't even pick my call. It's like he and his mother have connived to make my days bitter. What is so difficult in what I have asked of him? It is only right for him to listen to me. I know better. I have stayed longer on this planet and I know how the system works. The army is where Carlos needs to be. He has the looks, the mental and physical capacity. The fact that he has refused still keeps me in shock. I mean... How can you say no to such a juicy opportunity? How can you look progress in the eye and refuse it? I never knew a day would come when Carlos would be a pain in my arse."

"Hmm!" Sofia moves towards Santiago while speaking into the phone. She deliberately speaks loudly to make Santiago notice her. "Hello! Son. Are you still out? You know you need to be home in time for dinner, right?"

On the other end of the phone, Carlos sighs, "Yes Mama. And please tell Papa that he needs to stop calling me the entire time I am out spending with my friends. I am being responsible and will make it home in time for dinner.

Santiago listens to the conversation come to an end and mutters, "Was that Carlos? Did he say what time he will be home? He knows I hate it when he does not show his face at dinner."

Sofia rolls her eyes, "Why do you care?"

"Come on! Of course, you know I care," Santiago adds defensively.

"It doesn't seem like it," Sofia spits. "It's a good thing that Carlos gets to spend some time away from home. His dreams would have been drilled out of him if he had to listen to you every second of every day."

Santiago, catching his wife's sarcasm, adds, "You talk as if you aren't in support of him joining the army. You talk as if you had his back right from time. You ta..."

Sofia turns and glares at her husband, "Hey! Santiago Fuentes, I know your favorite pastime is trading blames but I won't stand here and watch you drag me into the mess you created by yourself. Of course, I supported your idea at that time because I thought it was a great idea. Talking with Carlos made me realize he was old enough to make his own decisions. I shifted ground because I recognized that Carlos had become a man. I had to let him make his choice. And if that choice includes not joining the army, then so be it!"

"Oh!" Santiago scoffs, "Now you sound all sanctimonious. I remember you asking me to push Carlos harder. You said if I pushed harder the boy with go with my idea. You stand here and deny it, Sofia. Well, it's expected."

"That's the very line you use when you want to guilt-trip me into accepting the blame for your mess up. This time I won't allow it Santiago. I won't at all," Sofia seethes gets ready to stomp away.

Before Sofia can leave, Santiago grabs at her arm, "Where do you think you are going? We haven't finished our discussion."

Sofia pulls herself free from Santiago's grip and shouts before leaving, "As far as I am concerned, we are done here!"

Santiago sighs, "So, my wife and kid are against me. What can a man do? And to think she was in support of Carlo joining the army and now she turns only to bite me. I am just a man that wants the best for my kid and if he doesn't see that and listens to me then it's a hopeless case."

He gets up and shouts before leaving the house, "I am going to watch the game at Steven's! They have discounts on their beer today!"

A few minutes later, Sofia stands by the door as she observes what is going on outside. Carlos and Selena are entering the front gate and seem in good spirits. As she watches her son approach, she cannot help but feel proud of the man he was becoming. Yes, he still had a lot of growing to do, both physically and mentally, but his heart was in the right place.

Sofia smiles as she holds the front door open for her son and his girlfriend, "Come on in you two.

Carlos looks around before asking, "Where's Papa?"

Sofia sighs, "Oh! Your dad went to watch a game. He will be back this evening."

"Steven's?" Carlos guesses.

When his mother does not answer, he relaxes a little. As long as his father wasn't here to lecture him again, he might as well enjoy it while it lasted!

Carlos sighs, "To think that he turned down the last invitation to come to watch me play a football match. He still hasn't gotten over the fact that I have gone this far without him. He is still angry that I refuse to go to the army despite his threats. Pappi is so unbending in his convictions which is not exactly a bad thing but sometimes he needs to be open to..."

"Can we stop this depressing talk and focus on happier memories?" Sofia asks. "Lest I forget, Selena of course you would like to see Carlo's baby pictures again. Let me get them for you."

Selena smiles as she watches Carlos' mother. She would never pass up an opportunity to show everyone her son's baby photos, no matter how embarrassing they might seem. She notices the frustrated expression on Carlos' face, reaches out, and squeezes his hand, "Babe, you have to let go. Your mother just wants to forget about you and your father constantly being at loggerheads. And for her, the best way to forget about that is by sharing pleasant memories about your childhood. You need to understand that you are her pride and joy. Although you might feel embarrassed about it sometimes, you should feel proud to have a Mama that cares so much about you."

"I know. She loves me to the ends of the earth. But I can't forget the fact that I was rejected by my father. Do you know how that feels? It's a heavy weight on my shoulders. The pain comes fresh every time I think I have moved on from the hurt," Carlos says.

"I don't claim to know but what I know is that everything happens for a reason," Selena smiles. "What your father wants you to become might be a stepping stone to greatness for you. You have to shut your eyes to the hurt and start seeing the limitless opportunities the decision you will make might open for you."

Carlos smiles back, "See why I like you so much? You make me see beauty in every pain. You make everything better. You bring order into the chaos of my life."

Sofia walks into the living room with a grey and white photo album in her hand. She holds it out towards Selena and says, "While you guys laugh over this, I will start with dinner. And Selena, you are staying as well. I am making a stew and there will be more than enough to go around."

Selena can't help but smile, "Your mom has always been so nice and warm. I always feel at home in her company."

"Yeah, she is something else, alright. But my dad…"

"Your dad isn't bad either," Selena offers. "I think their dispositions have more to do with their personalities. Your mama is an open and outgoing person so she exudes that aura whenever she is around people. She just can't help it. Your dad on the other hand is a more reserved man. I like to think that he is the observant and very introspective one. He sees the things that are not there and overthinks sometimes. That's just the way he is. It doesn't mean he is mean. You know he loves you and your siblings very much."

Carlos sighs, "It's amazing how you understand my father more than me. It's almost like you were born in this family. I know he loves me but it doesn't seem like that sometimes especially now that we are at loggerheads."

***

When Santiago returns later that evening, Sofia, with her arms crossed over her chest, glares at her husband, "I have something to tell you."

Santiago rubs his hands over his face, "What is it?"

"You know what it's about," Sofia says with a blank look on her face.

"It's about Carlos," Santiago rolls his eyes. You just want to ruin my mood now. Can we stop going back and forth on Carlos?"

"I don't think so," Sofia presses on. "He is our son no matter what. He is making us proud. You should really attend his last game. He wants you there. You know he does and it hurts him to know that you won't go simply because he does not want to follow in your footsteps."

"I never thought in my wildest dream that a day would come when my son and I would be total strangers," Santiago says thoughtfully.

"It doesn't have to be that way you know, if you can just swallow your pride," Sofia says softly.

"What about his pride?" Santiago hisses. "Why does it have to be my pride that has to be swallowed?"

"Hush!" Sofia whispers as Carlos is asleep upstairs. "Because you hurt him and because you are his father."

"It's so hard being a father to an almost-grown man. They might hate you for wanting the best for them," Santiago confirms.

"Do you really think if Carlos joins the army that would be his best life? I don't think so. As it starts now, it's evident that Carlos made the right choice. Your pride may not allow it but it's the truth."

Santiago scowls, "I am hurt too. He hurt me."

"How did he hurt you? By being successful at both school and football?" Sofia frowns.

Santiago sighs exasperated, "I tried reaching out to him but he wasn't having it. Do you know how many times I tried reaching out to him?"

"That's why you don't want to attend his game. Come on, that's childish. You are supposed to be the mature one," Sofia looks her husband in the eyes.

Santiago sighs, "I know. It's hard for me you know. I am controlled by my fears. I don't want my kid to end up like me that's why I try to make the choices that are right for them."

Sofia softens her voice and says calmly, "That's where you are wrong dear. A choice is called a choice because nobody else can make it for you. It's all in your hands. You can't dictate some else's path for them. They decide themselves. That's exactly what Carlos will do. He will choose himself and there's nothing wrong with that."

"Sofia, I am done talking about this. Done," Santiago says and heads towards the bedroom.

Carlos, awake and listening to his parents having yet another fight about him, covers his ears with his pillow. To try and forget about what his life was heading towards, Carlos thinks back to a time in his life where things seemed much less complex than they did right now.

"Good times…" Carlos whispered.

He thought back to the first time he joined a couple of his friends for a blunt under a bridge near the school. At that time, it seemed like the most exciting thing that had ever happened. Carlos was happy. He had friends now. A proper gang! Three cool girls from his school and four boys who all wore tracksuits and had gel in their hair and listened to hip hop. Carlos was 15 years old and finally felt like he was living his best teenage life.

It's autumn, and it's dark and damp. Carlos has a massive crush on one of the girls, Tamryn, who has long dark hair and smells like washing powder. When Carlos went to the shops with his mum, he tried to find out which washing powder it was. Maybe Dove? Carlos remembers them all mucking about, jumping over mud as they were stoned already.

Carlos felt much too shy to talk to Tamryn, let alone flirt with her, but still… They were walking together as part of the same group. Carlos felt a step closer to his big teenage ambition: getting a girlfriend.

The underpass where they were going to smoke the most exciting blunt of all time was on the other side of the river. It was about 9 pm. The wet bridge shimmered with car lights and glowing adverts rolled in a loop on the bus stop. A bus pulled up and a bunch of people got off. Carlos had hardly ever been out at night with friends before, but this felt safe and normal.

Then suddenly there was a commotion. A group of guys from the bus were rounding on the group. They were bigger than them and definitely older. They were men! One of them grabbed Carlos' newly-found friend and pushed him against the bridge wall so his upper body was leaning right back over the river below. The guys in Carlos' group start shouting. People were pushing each other. Carlos had never been mugged before. But then he had never gone for a blunt before, so maybe that was what it was always like? If not, he was unlucky. His first smoke under the bridge along with his first mugging.

He was scared that he was going to be caught in the ruckus, but now another man was ushering some of the group to one side. "Come with me," he said. "I'll keep you safe. Don't worry, don't worry, it'll be fine."

While three of the thugs, pretty big guys, seemed to be about to kill half the group, the fourth, much friendlier thug took the rest of us aside for a nice but quite awkward chat. "Don't worry, guys. Ignore my friends!" However, with one of my friends in the background being dangled over the bridge, it was hard to ignore.

Suddenly, the thug pointed at Carlos and ordered him to kiss Tamryn.

Carlos, completely dumb-founded did a double-take. He was being told to kiss the girl he was secretly in love with by a man whose friends are in the process of violently assaulting one of his friends! Carlos kept thinking Tamryn was going to say no, that she would look disgusted and laugh in my face, but she didn't. She just kind of moved towards Carlos, and Carlos moved towards her.

The thug was still there somewhere, creepily watching his successful teenage love match, but at that moment it was just Carlos and Tamryn. Carlos had never actually kissed someone he knew before, let alone someone he had got a massive crush on, but it was happening and under the strangest circumstances. They kissed. Not a peck on the cheek – this was a proper kiss, with tongues and everything.

Of course, it was the best kiss of his 15-year-old life. The damp air. The feel of her hair. Her lips. The smell of Dove. The vague awareness that there was a mugging happening somewhere out there. The kiss, which seemed to go on for ages, and was ridiculously good, unexpected fun.

Then it was over. Tamryn and Carlos stepped away from each other, smiling awkwardly. As quickly as they appeared, the thugs seemed to vanish into the night. Two of the group members were bleeding. They bottled one across the forehead, but it was not serious.

People take turns to finish the blunt on the reefer in the sickly yellow light of the underpass. The tiles and puddles threw their voices about. Carlos wanted to stand near Tamryn, catch her eye, he felt shy again. He didn't know how the next bit was meant to go. Still, he was buzzing. The night felt like magic. His love story had just begun, and it was a fucking great opening chapter…

Carlos let his thoughts wander back to the present, where he lay in his own bed. Luckily, the sound of his fighting parents has died down. With a smile on his face, he drifts off to sleep.

CHAPTER 8

Kobe is walking through the hood. He meets up with Reggie and embraces him. During the embrace, Reggie slips a wad of cash into his pocket.

"What's up bruh?" Reggie says. "Y'all kicked some ass the other day. I know your pops is proud. Don't get it twisted though...our 1985 Championship team can still whip your ass."

Kobe continues walking away smiling, "Not a chance Reggie...we got Dre Banks!"

Reggie smiles shaking his head, "And we had Bo... Yo, I put a little something in there for you. Be safe bruh."

Kobe looks at his pocket and sticks his hand into it as he continues walking.

A short while later, Kobe walks into his modest apartment where the kids, Zoey and Marley are playing video games. He goes over and hugs them then walks into the kitchen where Toni, his mom, is cooking. He tastes some of the cooking on the spoon.

"Oh no you didn't," Toni says with mock anger.

"It's so good," Kobe replies sheepishly.

"Well, it will be done in ten minutes," Toni says while taking the spoon from Kobe.

"I gotta go," Kobe apologizes.

Toni frowns, "Where you going, Kobe?"

"To see my friends…" Kobe says vaguely.

"Well don't be too late," Toni warns. "I need you to watch the kids tomorrow. I have to work."

"Working the weekend?" Kobe asks.

Toni sighs while still stirring the pot, "Yes, working the weekend."

Kobe discreetly takes the cash out of his pocket and puts it in a cookie jar.

He kisses his mom on the cheek, "Okay mama, I'll see you later."

"And you be safe out there. You know I can't sleep until I know you're home safely," Toni warns.

"Yes, Mama," Kobe grabs his backpack and leaves.

Toni mutters, "This boy should keep the hell outta trouble. I don't want him living like his pops."

***

Kobe finds himself at a party downtown with his bag pack. He talks to a group of boys who are smoking weed and talking loudly. He moves from there and talks to other people. He is searching for Reggie and as soon as he sees him, he approaches him.

"Hey!" Kobe calls. "Man. Dunno you be out here. I thought you were busy doing some other things, man. Like tightening some loose ends or shit."

Reggie, with a cigarette, puffs the smoke into the air, "Man! I just came here to loosen up. You get the money I gave you?"

Kobe nods, "Yeah, I gave it to my Mom. But why don't you ever tell me where the money comes from?"

"You just continue being a good boy and you will soon be up the ladder. You have your father's spirit boy. I see your old man in you," Reggie smiles.

"Nah!" Kobe winces. "I ain't following my pops footsteps. If I am, I am gonna end up just like him and my momma would die. I can't risk my momma dying on me."

"Boy!" Reggie laughs. "Then you'd better be sure to stay far away from anything your father brings your way. The moment you get into the game it means you could risk anything including your own Momma. Life ain't taught you nothing yet?"

"Life has taught me to be careful," Kobe frowns.

Reggie scoffs, "Really! That's all you got? Careful? You got to be kidding me."

"I don't know about you Reggie but in the game, I think you are playing this that lesson comes in handy," Kobe confirms.

"Kobe! Your Pops didn't teach you. A few bruises here and there will," Reggie says.

"How do you mean?" Kobe asks, confused.

"Have fun and make sure you get home safe…" Reggie says as he walks away from Kobe.

Hours later, Kobe, half-drunk struggles to enter his house. He makes so much noise that he wakes his Momma.

Toni is irritated as she opens the door, "I raised you better than this boy. What's with you going out and getting all drunk? It's midnight and you are causing a lot of commotion."

"Naw!" Kobe smiles. "I ain't causing a ruckus momma. You see anybody out here? Naw! It's barely midnight momma. What are you making a fuss about?"

"Just look at yourself," Toni says, disgusted. "What will your younger ones say? Young Marley and Zoey look up to you. What you gonna tell them?"

"Yikes!" Kobe complains. "Momma, your voice is so loud it's causing the bells to ring in my head. Momma chill, Marley and Zoey are sleeping. You wouldn't want to wake them up now."

Toni shakes her head, "Something is wrong Kobe. Since you picked that call in the cab when you went to see your pops you have been acting strange. I pray heavens you aren't involved in any crooked stuff."

"Not now momma. My head is aching. I just wanna sleep not receive some lecture. I am a man and should be treated as..." Kobe slurs.

"Man you say?" Toni cuts him off. "If you want to be treated like a man then you start acting like one. Kobe Briggs!"

"Aw! Man just wants to be free from silly expectations. I am damn tired," Kobe says as he drifts off to sleep.

A few hours later, Kobe wakes up with a nagging headache and he winces as his momma draws the curtains back.

"Whoa! The lights Momma," Kobe groans as he shields his eyes.

"You better get up, Kobe," Toni says sternly.

Kobe sighs, "It's like the devil is throwing a party in my head. My head is shaking. Argh!"

Toni rolls her eyes, "I don't know what you have been up to son but whatever it is just pray it doesn't end in a bad way for you."

"Not now ma," Kobe groans. "Not now. I just woke up and I am in no state for lectures. All I am doing is trying to do is finding some peace. That ain't so wrong Momma."

"Whatever you do please do not end up like your father," Toni instructed. "Breakfast is ready. Come eat."

"After I am done brushing," Kobe winces. "My mouth stinks."

"Yes it does," Toni says and turns away from her son before he can see the tear rolling down her cheek.

"I am sorry Ma," Kobe says. "I know how disappointed you must be in me. I don't know what came over me… Things… Things sometimes just get under my skin and I have to let go."

When his mother does not reply, he shuffles towards the bathroom to wet his face before his sisters see him in such a sorry state.

Minutes later, at the table Zoey looks at her brother, "Kobe! What about College? I overheard Marley saying you weren't interested. I thought you loved school."

"Umm... Eh... Of course, I love school. Well, it's just..." Kobe didn't quite know what to say.

Marley cuts in, "Kobe realizes school ain't worth it these days. The streets pay though."

Toni gasps as her eyes widen in shock, "Marley! You been hanging out with those street kids too much. Who put that silly idea into your head?"

"Momma!" Marley adds, "It's true. You see Reggie. Reggie sure makes more bread than some doctors."

"Nah! Man... The streets don't pay nobody. It always ends up messed up. It ain't worth it Marley," Kobe says.

"It always ends up blood and dirty kinda reminds me of pops," Zoey chimes. "The Cops were always calling at our house whenever there's a shoot down."

"Pops was a real nigga though. I miss him," Silence greets the table at Marley's last statement.

After a few seconds, Kobe shakes his head, "Nah! I don't miss him."

"Come on guys, let's eat," Toni tries to change the subject.

"About College Zoey," Kobe tries again, "I am sure getting into it someday. It's just that with pops gone I have to settle some things and make sure you all are comfortable." He pinches Zoey's cheek lightly.

"I love you, Kobe. We love you," Zoey smiles.

Kobe pauses as he gets emotional, "I love you guys too Pumpkin. Come on, eat your food."

Marley digs into her meal, "Momma, tastes great as always. That reminds me, when are we going to see pops?"

"Not now Marley," Toni freezes.

"What do you mean not now, Momma?" Marley pushes. "I want to see pops. It's been a while. You do not let us go anymore. Kobe doesn't even go anymore."

"Marley!" Kobe scolds. "Can we talk about this later?"

"As usual," Marley snaps, "Later means it will be swept under the carpet never to be remembered. I am sick and tired of this. Pops wasn't perfect but he was a real man. He fought for what he believed in and..."

Kobe, now clearly angry, spits, "Shut your mouth, Marley. What do you know about beliefs? What do you freaking know about rights and wrongs? Marley, tell me!" He hits the table and rises to his feet.

Toni, shocked by Kobe outburst, gasps, "Kobe..."

"No ma," Kobe demands. "I am tired of his whining and complaining. He doesn't know shit. He doesn't know what pops has done to us. He doesn't know the shit we are into. He doesn't know anything."

Zoey starts crying, "Stop! You guys should just stop. You are making me nervous."

Marley continues grunting, "Nobody seems to understand pops. You all judge him."

"You say what?" Kobe seethes. "Speak up! Speak up if you aren't a freaking coward like your pops."

"You don't care about pops," Marley shouts. "You are just a bunch of selfish bastards."

Kobe, who fully understands the situation that got his pops into jail from the get-go, can now see that his siblings do not share the same thoughts. Yes, he wants his siblings to love their father. After all, it is the only thing that seems to keep them going. The fact that they might still see their father come out of jail someday. But as far as Kobe is concerned, his pops had made the decision as to who was more important a long time ago. If he had chosen his family over his drug-dealings, Kobe would have still given him a chance. Kobe feels as if his mind and heart is fighting against each other. One part of him wants his siblings to hate their father just as Kobe does. But the other half of him wants to love his father just like his siblings do. To Kobe, it is frustrating as he does not know how to put his feelings into words. Since he is seen as "the man of the house" while his father is away, showing any kind of emotion might make his siblings think of him as an untrustworthy person.

Kobe reaches out and slaps Marley hard across the face, "Bitches? You need to be grounded for a month."

Marley holds his face in pain, "What?"

Toni stands between the siblings, "Stop it you two. Marley! To your room now."

As Marley rushes off to her room, Toni puts her hands on her hips, "What just happened? Kobe are you sure you're alright? That outburst was uncalled for. And to hit your sister… I don't even know what to say!"

Zoey sniffs, "Kobe, is something wrong? You try to hide it, but you forget that I am your mother. I can see right through you into your troubled heart."

Kobe runs his hand down his face, "No. Nothing is wrong. I am just stressed. I need to rest."

Toni touches his face, "You can talk to me boy. We can fix anything that's wrong. I am here for you. I know you want all of us to see you as a pillar of strength but I know you are still a young man. You don't have to carry so much responsibility with you. No one expects you to."

"I am fine, Momma. Really! I am. I have lost my appetite, Ma. I need to run. I am running late and I need to get to school. These last few days are going to be brutal," Kobe lies.

"Want me to pack some food for you?" Toni asks, deeply troubled by her son's strange behavior.

"No ma. I will eat at school. Don't worry," Kobe kisses his Momma on the head and kisses Zoey on the cheek before he heads out the front door.

While staring after him, Toni murmurs, "Something is not right with Kobe. I can feel it in my bones."

"I can see it," Zoey adds. "Kobe has something up his sleeve. Momma, I don't want anything to hurt him. I am scared for him."

"I will get to the bottom of this," Toni says thoughtfully.

***

Kobe is leaning against a pillar in a seedy part of town as he listens to Reggie talking to someone on the phone.

"What's up?" Reggie asks the person on the other side of the line. "You watched the match yesterday?"

"Yeah! Dre Banks made a great move. He saved the day," the voice says.

Reggie scoffs, "You think?"

"I..." the caller hesitates.

Reggie clears his throat, "Listen, I hope you are calling me with some good news. So, have you delivered the package?"

"Emm... I was supposed to…" The caller hesitates again.

Reggie raises his voice, "Supposed to?"

"Yeah!" The caller adds. "My mother was sick and I had to see her to the hospital. It delayed my plans."

"What the hell?" Reggie fumes. "Mixing family with street business? Do you know what you have just done?"

"It ain't that serious man," the caller responds. "I will have them delivered today. It was just a little delay."

"Shit!" Reggie curses. "A little what? Do you know what you are saying? I had given my word to that squad. I told them that it had already been delivered as I promised. I did that because I trusted you to get the job done before they came calling. What you are saying now is the parcel is still with you?"

"Umm... Yes, it is Reggie but I promise..." the caller begs.

"Your words mean nothing to me," Reggie spits. "You have made a mess of a simple task. Oh! I miss your father. I thought you were just like him. I thought you were driven, street smart but it turns out you are just your Mama's boy."

"What's this fuss about a single missed delivery?" the caller responds. "In all the time I worked for you, did I ever miss a delivery? This time, there was an emergency. I couldn't just leave my mother."

"That's a lot of story that makes no sense to me," Reggie snaps. "It's always duty before family. Your father understood that. That understanding protected him from a lot."

"Protected him from what exactly?" the caller is clearly angry, "These stupid street runs are what caused my family pain all these years. It's what put my father behind bars. Briggs, you and your men are just a bunch of liars. You said you would protect him but you didn't. You abandoned him when the cops came calling. You are..."

"Your dad owed and he had to pay his dues," Reggie states. "That's just how the system works. We couldn't help him."

"Of course, you couldn't help him because you have your own mess to clean up," the caller continues. "Nobody is really as concerned about you the way you are about yourself. That's the simple thing pops didn't understand. He chose the street over family now look what that got him."

Reggie fumes, "Oh! Shut up! He wanted a better life for you and your mother.

"If this is the better life then I ain't living it anymore. Reggie, I am done. I ain't doing this," the caller adds.

Reggie laughs a deep throaty laugh, "You wish, you wish. You can't come in and leave at will. Like it or not, you are part of the gang. You have stepped into your father's shoes and there's no escape."

"I choose what to do with my life. I am done filling anybody's shoes," the caller presses on.

"You are aiming for trouble," Reggie warns. "Do you know the implication of that statement? You are a part of this syndicate. You can't step out."

"Briggs I am completely done," the caller says one last time. "You want somebody to work for you? Go get my father from prison."

Reggie cuts the calls and looks over to Kobe, who seems horrified at what he has just heard.

Without flinching, Reggie smiles, "You see, it could have been you on the other side of the phone there. Same as you. Also has a father in prison. Only difference between you and this guy is that your father is making sure that you don't have to do his dirty work. Whereas this poor dude needs to continue where his father left off. And from the looks of it, he's out…"

"You mean… He sells dope?" Kobe asks, confused.

Reggie laughs, "Hey, man! Where do you think the dough comes from that I so selflessly give you and your Momma?"

Kobe has always suspected that the cash his father made sure Reggie gave him every once in a while came from shady dealings but having it confirmed still sends shivers down his spine.

Reggie suddenly seems like he is in a rush, "I gotta go, man." He gives Kobe a hug, which is a bit unusual.

Kobe feels the left side of his jacket pocket move a little, but before he can look what it is, Reggie gives a high pitched laugh, which distracts Kobe.

"See ya, Man!" Reggie says and sprints off.

Kobe turns to make his way back home.

As soon as he walks through the front door, Toni confronts him, "Where have you been?"

"What you mean? I was at school and then went to see Reggie," Kobe answers.

"Reggie?" Toni spits. I knew something was up. My gut don't lie. This boy wanna go the way of his pops. Hanging out with Reggie, that low life!"

Toni cannot hold her anger in anymore and starts ripping at Kobe's jacket.

"Momma, stop!" Kobe pleads.

Within seconds, a small plastic wrapper falls out of Kobe's left pocket and onto the floor. Both Kobe and Toni stares at the wrapper while both of them already knows what the inside of the wrapper contains.

"Reggie…" Kobe whispers in disbelief.

"What have you done?" Toni wails. "You promised me, again and again, you won't go down the same path as your pops! You promised me!"

"I can explain, Momma. Just let me explain. This is not me! I did not do this!" Kobe says, shocked.

"Explain what?" Toni spat. "That you've gone the ways of your pops despite my incessant pleas. After all the pains your pops caused us you still chose his path."

Kobe tried calming his mother down, "I am sorry, Ma, you need to listen to me! I would never…"

Toni, visibly shaken and not about to listen to her son, shouts, "Sorry? You think sorry can fix this? You think sorry is gonna stop those hoodlums from coming after you, after us?"

Kobe does not know how to explain that it was Reggie who had planted the dope on him in the first place, "Momma, I don't know…"

Toni, with tears in her eyes, yells, "You don't know? You don't understand the men you are dealing with. They are cold-blooded men. You really shouldn't have gotten yourself involved in the first place."

"I will fix this, Momma. I will. Please don't cry," Kobe says, close to tears himself. "This was not me! It was Reggie. Please, Momma, you have to believe me!"

Toni looks into her son's eyes and for the first time, she realizes that her son might be innocent. She composes herself and seethes, "That bastard. That bloody bastard. We should report to the cops."

Kobe shakes his head, "No momma. The cops will get me too. They will send me to jail. I don't want to spend my time in jail. I don't want to be like pops. I would love to live a better life and be a better person."

Toni frowns, "But you just said it wasn't you!"

Kobe looked at the floor, "The money Reggie sends… It is dope money, Momma… We are living off pop's dope money…"

CHAPTER 9

Dre is in his bedroom where the walls are covered with posters of black quarterbacks. He goes over to his desk where there's a hand-written note that contains the word "MixTape." The note has a list of songs beside the names of Noah, Kobe, Carlos and Dre.

With his head to one side, Dre sighs into his pillow as he thinks back to the stories his grandmother and a younger friend used to tell him when he visited them. His grandmother's friend, Carter, always had a piece of himself to share and he never held back on the details.

"Like many of my generation," Carter had said, "I was a mixtape-making fiend in high school. I spent long hours honing my craft, carefully considering the transitions between songs, striving to give each side of the cassette its own cohesive mood, timing out my tracklists to the second so the final song of the side wouldn't get cut off. I made tapes for friends and even family, but mostly I made tapes for girls. I wasn't the first teenage boy to use music as a kind of emotional cheat, a way of expressing feelings I wasn't mature enough to put into words and hopefully stirring up reciprocal feelings in my intended listener. It may even have worked a time or two. What to do once she took the headphones off was another story."

"Don't you go filling his head with what you were up to when you were his age," Dre's grandmother would warn, but would continue to listen out of pure interest.

Carter continued, "I've given out dozens, maybe even hundreds, of mixtapes over the years, but as far as I can recall, I've only received a few in return. In my freshman year of high school, I had a crush on a ballerina named Jenny. After one awkward walk on the waterfront, I could tell she wasn't interested, but she did want to be friends, so she made me a mix for my birthday. It was weird—the A-side was mostly mood songs getting with your emotions and side B was all about feeling the beats and snapping your fingers and bobbing your head.

"I agree with you there! Music is a language all on its own!" Dre had said with enthusiasm as he listened to Carter tell his story.

"There you go!" Carter smiled before he pushed on, "By far the most significant mixtape anyone ever gave me came from a girl I never dated or even knew that well. Amanda was close with my college girlfriend Natalie. I hung out with her a lot in those years, but she was always a bit inscrutable to me. She spoke quietly and sparingly. Her eyes were sleepy but watchful. She wore overalls and got her tongue pierced. All I knew about her background was that she came from a religious family. We were never in any classes together, and I'm not sure what she studied. I remember having at least one intense private conversation with her but not what we actually talked about. I could never completely decide if I found her sexy. I was surprised to get a mixtape from Amanda, although I'd made at least one for her. It was a more outgoing gesture than I'd come to expect from her. The mix itself was surprising, too, in a variety of ways. First was the fact that it had cover art: a photo, presumably clipped from a magazine, of a boy sitting in a wheat field looking up at the sky, his face shrouded in shadow. The tracklist was typed out and pasted to the back of the jacket. The care and formality of it impressed me. I'd never gone beyond scrawling the names of songs in erasable pen. Amanda's handwriting only appears on the spine. She'd given her mix a title: "The Broccoli Mix." Looking at it now, I have no idea what it's supposed to mean. Did I know then? Probably not. On the surface, the choice of songs wasn't all that remarkable. Most were highly familiar, though not necessarily staples of my record collection. The real surprise was how the music made me feel. For years, I'd been invoking the power of the mix to cast a spell on the ones I wanted. But until then I'd never been under that spell myself. "Sh-boom," "Let's Get It On," "Rock with You," "Close to Me," "Sunday Girl," "In Your Eyes," even "Why Don't You Write Me"—these were seductive songs. Weren't they? Was it possible Amanda meant them that way? All I knew for sure was that I felt seduced."

"Carter, I am warning you…" Dre's grandmother said but attentively kept listening to know what happened next.

Ready to continue, Carter sighed, "I was aware I was reading into things, selectively at that. The idea that my girlfriend's best friend was trying to send me a message seemed farfetched, but I couldn't shake it, especially when I listened to the last two songs on the tape. The tape ran out before the song ended, deepening my sense that something had been left unsaid, unresolved. It was such a nagging feeling that I made what I now recognize as a dipshit move: I brought it up with my girlfriend. I think I prefaced what was on my mind with some mealy-mouthed qualifier like, "If I didn't know better…" Lucky for me, all Natalie did was laugh. The idea was preposterous, not worth even a moment's consideration. I never said anything about it to anyone again. Natalie broke up with me at the end of our sophomore year. Amanda started a relationship with the guy she would go on to marry. I haven't spoken to her since we graduated. I'm not on social media, so she isn't even a residual presence in my life. Needless to say, I don't have a cassette deck anymore. I still think about that tape, though, because of the handful of songs that gave me what I've always longed for as a listener: the thrill of discovery. It was embarrassing, getting so hot and bothered over Amanda's mixtape. It still makes me squirm a little knowing that what I heard in it was almost certainly a figment of my imagination. I can see how I was projecting. I thought mixtapes were for making people love you. Time moves on, and what lasts is the love of the music."

"Love of the music…" Dre murmurs to himself as his thoughts snap back to reality.

Sighing, he gets up, picks up his headphones and the speaker, takes the note with the list of songs and puts it in his pocket. He walks out of his room.

"I am off…" Dre says as he makes a beeline towards the front door, hoping his parents won't stop him to ask questions.

"Where you off to?" Otis asks as his eyes leave the television screen.

"Me and the guys are heading to a party," Dre replies vaguely.

Otis sighs, "Be careful son."

"Are you giving him the talk?" Cheryl frowns and looks at her husband while she sits on a couch across from him.

Dre squints, "The talk?"

"Ya, the talk…" Otis says in a serious tone.

Dre bursts out into laughter, "Dad, I am good."

"Dre," Cheryl responds, "The Talk has nothing to do with birds and bees. It is about surviving police encounters, being aware of your rights and learning how to live within a complex, systemic, centuries-old framework of race-based prejudice, violence and discrimination."

"Dre," Otis adds, "It's about keeping you safe in a world too often hostile to the presence of you because of your skin color. We've had this talk before...We have but I feel obligated to have this talk every time you leave the safety of this house."

"Why does this have to be so hard?" Dre complains. "We just won the championship the other day. This isn't right."

"The scars from slavery, discriminatory housing policies and the war on drugs have all contributed to the pain and poverty our people have endured. We must never forget," Cheryl warns.

"I get it but do you really think it matters?" Dre moves a few more inches towards the front door. "If they want to hurt me they will. I saw the video of the Chicago cop shooting a seventeen-year-old sixteen times...most after the teen lay on the ground."

"That's right..." Otis shrugs, "And I grew up with the Rodney King beating fresh in mind."

"Dre, please remember how to behave in the presence of police, not to mitigate potential harm. No sudden movements, don't question why you're being stopped, comply with all verbal commands, never raise your voice. Please Dre," Cheryl continues to beg.

"And Dre," Otis raises his brow, "Blasting Ice Cube's and N.W.A.'s Fu… The police might not be the best choice for the ride."

Dre feels the note with his friend's favorite songs of all time burning an invisible hole in his pocket, "Wait what, now you're telling me what music to listen to?"

"Dre, the system needs to be fixed," Cheryl continues. "You're right, it is unfair to burden you kids with these responsibilities."

Not about to listen to his parents nagging voices any longer, Dre waves, "I'm out of here."

"Be safe Dre!" Cheryl calls after him as she hears the front door slam shut.

"I don't get why he's angry though," Otis looks at his wife. "Dude is just like a ticking bomb ready to explode any minute."

"Can you blame him?" Cheryl frowns.

"Meaning?" Otis crosses his arms over his chest.

"Never mind…" Cheryl says as she turns her attention back to the television.

A few moments pass before Cheryl's thoughts drift back to a recent conversation she had with Dre. They were in the kitchen and Dre was helping her prepare dinner. In the absence of Otis, Cheryl thought it might be a good idea to nudge Dre into opening up about his teenage feelings and thoughts about life in general.

"Pass me the salt please," Cheryl had started the conversation off on a light note.

Dre passes the salt, "Here Ma."

"Thanks… So what you been up to lately? It's been a while we've been in the same place together. Nowadays it seems like you're avoiding me," Cheryl coordinated the conversation in the direction she wanted it to go.

Dre shrugged, "Avoiding you ma? No. But avoiding dad? Yes. Plus I always need to be at practice and I have school work too. I am aiming to come out top of the class as well as play in the next season. I have been very busy."

"You're doing your best, dear," Cheryl sighed.

"I wish dad could say the same," Dre answered. "He only sees the wrong especially with my determination to play as a quarterback in the NFL."

"He is quite proud of you nonetheless. Your father loves you but..." Cheryl started.

"He certainly has a weird way of showing it," Dre looked at the meat on the cutting board, ready to become a delicious meat pie.

"You see, the definition of love for fathers is different from that of mothers," Cheryl explained. "Fathers see love as security, protection, defense. That's the way they interpret it. Your father's love for you is seen in the way he protects you. He wants to shield you from the harsh realities that life as an African-American brings. It isn't his fault. Which parent wouldn't be overly protective of their kids especially if they knew that just by the skin color the child could be murdered at any minute? Please understand."

"Ma, you talk like you don't know things have changed and are still changing. Some years back blacks couldn't play in the national team let alone play as quarterbacks. Now, the numbers of black players and quarterbacks are relatively high. In the next five to six years I assure you that skin color wouldn't be an issue for us anymore," Dre protested.

Cheryl stopped what she was doing and looked Dre in the eyes, "I believe that things are changing and will keep changing but we can't risk the time it will take son. Five, six years is a long time. What if things get worse? What if..."

Dre cut in, "What if? That sounds a lot like Dad… His negativity is rubbing off on you. I am aware of your fears but it doesn't change my stance. I will shoot for the stars even if the sky doesn't like my skin. The color of my skin doesn't change anything, Ma."

"You know what, son?" Cheryl sighed. "It's your life. Do what you want if it makes you happy."

"What's that thing you were saying about how mothers express their love? Dre smiled as he winked at his mother.

Cheryl chuckled, "They let you do what you want to do while praying that it doesn't kill you."

Dre picked up a knife and started slicing some onions, "We are almost done here."

"Yeah! Just a little more and we are done," Cheryl agreed as she opened the pot and stirred.

"The aroma has set my stomach on fire!" Dre commented, his mouth watering for his mother's cooking.

"Let's hope you don't get burnt before the food reaches the table," Cheryl warned playfully.

An hour later, Cheryl, Otis and Dre were sitting at the dinner table when the first comment was made.

"Food tastes a little too spicy," Otis said as he pinched the bridge of his nose.

"That's because I added a little too much spice," Dre added sarcastically.

Otis dropped his cutlery, "Can you ever get anything right?"

Cheryl gasped, "Otis! That's a little too harsh."

"I don't care," Otis says as he moves his plate to one side.

Dre looked at the food on his plate, "Ma, never mind."

"I have lost my appetite," Otis said as he shifted his chair backwards and got up to leave.

Dre frowned, "Come on, Dad, it's just a little spice. It isn't too much to cause you to lose your appetite."

"You know what?" Otis said as he looked at his son with fury blazing in his eyes. "I have to get this off my chest."

"What exactly?" Dre demanded.

"When are you planning to stop playing for the local team?" Otis asked.

"Never, Dad," Dre spat.

Otis' eyes widened as he looked at Cheryl, "Never? Can you hear your son?"

"Otis, please just drop it. Now is not the time," Cheryl begged.

"When is the time Cheryl?" Otis demanded. "When he goes off to get killed?"

Dre, exasperated, answered, "Dad! You are acting so paranoid. Get killed? The hell! Am I on a battlefield?"

"You think everything is a joke don't you?" Otis seethed. "I want you to stop pursuing that dream of being a quarterback for the NFL. That means you can have to stop playing for the local team."

"Otis!" Cheryl gasped in disbelief, "He is a gifted player. The coach said so."

"It doesn't matter what the coach said. He isn't the head of my house," Otis slapped his hand on the table.

Dre stood up to his full height to address his father, "Of all the demands you've made of me I have never for once refused. I have lived all my life in your shadow. I have done all you asked of me without a single protest but there's so much one can take. I am no longer a child anymore. You cannot push me around. I choose what to do with my life sorry if you don't approve because I seriously don't need your approval. The only approval I need is mine and mine alone."

Cheryl, not quite knowing how to save the situation, protested, "Dre! You shouldn't talk to your father that way. Show him some respect."

Dre lowered his voice before storming out, "Respect is earned ma not given for free."

"Come on let's finish our food," Cheryl said as she felt and confused by the sudden outburst.

Otis goaned, "Finish what?"

Otis sat back down at the table and looked at his wife, "You know what? Let's continue this conversation. Let me make you understand why I am being like this. Do you know how the system is towards young black players? They do not give us breathing space. They always want to snuff our lives out just because we have a little too much melanin. You see why I want Dre to quit? I can't take my son dying on me."

Cheryl sighed, "Nobody is dying on anybody Otis. You have a lot of hrt in your head. Dre is safe."

"Safe?" Otis shouted. "Are you kidding me? No black man is ever safe. Now that stubborn boy of ours has decided to be more conspicuous than ever by playing for the team. One day what we have been dreading may just happen. Have you seen his teammates? He sticks out like a sore thumb.”

“But...” Cheryl protested.

Dre burst back into the room, “Could you just all stop it! Please, Dad, Not now. I am exhausted.”

Otis ignored his son’s plea, “You really don't know what you're doing. You should be as inconspicuous as possible like the rest of us.”

“Like the rest of you who have decided to live small lives. I don't want that for myself. I...” Dre caught himself before he could say something he might regret later. “I need to clear my head…” Dre made sure to slam the door extra hard as he retreated to his room.

Otis looked at Cheryl, “That he is hell-bent on ruining himself is what gets me every time.”

“You know that isn't true,” Cheryl commented. “Dre is a golden child. A rare one. How many boys do you see hell-bent on making difference in their lives and he is doing it the right way? Cut him some slack, Otis.”

“Cut him some slack?” Otis scoffed. “Am I the bad guy here? Cheryl, sometimes I think you understand and at other times I think you don't. You have chosen to side with Dre which is up to you.”

"I am not taking sides," Cheryl said defensively. "I am just saying you should let him be. He is quite determined and you can't stop him."

"I can't stop him because he has you supporting him. You're his mom, so you won't really understand," Otis spat.

Cheryl, angry at the comment, answered, "Are you saying because I am his mom I don't understand the struggles our people face? Did you really just say that? Otis, your attitude is quite shocking."

Otis threw his hands in the air, "You are already jumping to conclusions. I didn't say that."

"But you just said it," Cheryl confirmed. "What is wrong with you Otis? You don't see the shining light in your son. What kind of a man are you? Any father would be proud to have a son like Dre who has chosen well. Do you know how many boys his age have taken to the streets? Do you know how many have chosen the wrong way? Dre has chosen to make something meaningful out of his life but you fight him because he wants to be a quarterback?"

"Unbelievable!" Cheryl ran her hands over her face, "I can't believe that you are trying to rub your insecurities on us. You have been afraid to live Otis. You have been afraid to truly live. All you do is exist. I see you bury your dreams under a pile of baggage. You saw the impossibilities in every little thing and you let that drag you down. You are not a happy man Otis. You are just a man waiting for time to pass so you would cross over to the other side. It's pathetic Otis but what is more pathetic is that you want to drag your son to the death that is eating you up inside. That is certainly the most pathetic thing ever."

"What?" Otis boiled over with anger. "You talk to me like you aren't aware of how hard I tried to live my dreams. But the system is working against you not for you. Nobody understands me. Nobody at all. My fears are not unfounded. They are not at all. I just hope that boy listens before it's too late."

"Cheryl? Cheryl..."

Cheryl's mind snaps back to where Otis is still sitting in front of the television.

"Cheryl, are you even listening?" Otis demands.

"I… my mind must have shifted gear there for a few minutes… What were you saying?" Cheryl shakes her head to try and get the unpleasant memory from her mind.

CHAPTER 10

The friends have all met at Eddie's convenience store. Noah is sitting in his car while Dre, Kobe, and Carlos enter the convenience store. They are playing music and are enjoying the moment. The store owner seems very agitated.

"Turn down the music, only 3 at a time," the store owner grumbles as he points towards a sign reading 3 students at a time.

Kobe bursts out into laughter pointing at himself, then Dre, and finally Carlos, "1, 2, 3... What's the problem?"

"You people are too loud!" the store owner says again.

Kobe gets agitated, "You people?"

Dre sighs, "Just grab the stuff and let's go. He doesn't want us in here."

"No but he will take our money," Carlos adds.

"And we keep giving it to him," Dre concludes.

Kobe finishes taking what they're buying and goes to the counter. He reaches into his pocket and flips the store owner the finger. The guys all laugh as Kobe throws the money for the goods on the counter and they leave.

"Keep the change," Kobe scoffs as he exits.

The guys leave the store and walk over to where Noah's car is parked. They look into the car and see Noah with his head on the steering wheel. They pause before entering the car and look at one another with concern.

"I got mad love for that dude," Kobe confides.

"Real-life bruh," Dre nods.

"Straight up mamba to even continue playing football," Carlos thinks back to the game Noah had recently played.

Noah looks out at the guys and rolls down the window, "Let's go...its time to turn it up!"

The guys get into the car. Carlos in the front, Kobe and Dre in the back.

Noah looks at his friends, "Kobe, you got the stuff?"

Kobe smiles hold up a blunt then runs it across his nose smelling it.

"Carlos, you got the juice?" Noah asks again.

Carlos smiles and holds up a couple of bottles of alcohol, "Check!"

They all start chanting and dancing in unison, "Hey, Hey, Hey, Hey!"

Noah smiles, "Dre, you got the mixtape?"

Dre plays a beat, "I got this, y'all life in music is on this tape. Check."

Noah sings a verse from Queen, "No time for losers we are the champions of the world. Lets make this a night to remember. You got this Dre?"

"Ya, I got this...bring it in fellas," Dre says with adrenaline starting to build up in his system.

The guys do a makeshift huddle in the car and bring their hands into the middle. One hand on top of the other.

Dre laughs, "It feels good to go out a champion."

The guys all agree with nods.

"Tonight is our night..." Dre continues, "A night to remember."

"I just want to say..." Carlos mentions "I have probably played my last game of football. I am just glad we did it right."

"What are you saying right now?" Dre asks, confused.

"I am saying it's time..." Carlos says with a serious face. "It's time for me to get on with my life. I am eighteen. I am going to join the military and marry Selena."

"Hold up..." Dre puts his hands in the air, "You're the valedictorian... accepted to Harvard."

Kobe laughs seemingly sarcastically, "Why you even coming to this party? Did Selena even let you out?"

Carlos rolls his eyes, "I want to chill with my brothers tonight."

Kobe looks at his friends dreamily, "I love me some Selena... not your Selena. I am talking Gomez bro... Wizards of Waverly."

Dre laughs, "You're kind of young for all this?"

"She is the one I want to be with for the rest of my life," Carlos confides.

Noah interrupts and changes the topic, "Dre, can we get some music now?"

Dre nods, "I have y'all life in music on the mix. Everyone got a mood track, everyone got an anthem."

"Mood?" Kobe asks. "We don't need to be in our feelings tonight. The only mood is to turn up."

Noah gets a call which he answers, "Okay, hold up for a sec... they're going... text me the address."

Noah ends the call and turns to Kobe, "Well, we have a party to go to now! I am just waiting on the address. Kobe, pass me the blunt."

Kobe passes the weed to Noah.

Kobe hesitates and says, "We sparking it now?"

"Nah... You know if we get stopped, They ain't saying nothing to me," Noah mumbles.

"Not cool," Dre sighs.

Kobe laughs mockingly, "If we get stopped, they probably going to think you're our UBER driver."

"It's real life," Noah confirms. "My dad was a cop. I know how they think."

"Like my dad says," Dre adds, "We are much more likely to be suspected than respected."

Carlos shakes his head, "Not tonight fellas. Tonight's our night..."

The guys all chime in in unison, "No time for losers we are the champions of the world."

"Dre, whats on that mixtape for me?" Noah asks as he stops singing.

"I got some Juiceworld," Dre suggests.

"His freestyle is crazy," Kobe says, excited.

Carlos breaks out into a freestyle about Selena while they guys are laughing and having a great time.

As they calm down again, Carlos speak, "Seriously though, we keep losing too many brothers to drugs and guns."

"Don't forget jail," Kobe adds. "A lot of brothers in jail."

"Jail is a choice though..." Dre suggests.

Kobe frowns, "Choice? You tripping on that Jail or Yale shit. It ain't no choice. It's God's Plan."

Carlos lowers his head, "Come on bruh, it's no plan of God to keep our peeps down. Do we not all have one Father?"

Carlos looks around the car at the guys seem to get their attention, "Did not one God create us? Why do we profane the covenant of our ancestors by being unfaithful to one another? Malachi 2 verse 10."

"Preach, my brother," Kobe nods his head in agreement.

"Amen!" Dre agrees. Though I don't know what I believe anymore?"

"Be strong and courageous," Carlos suggests. "Do not be afraid or terrified because of them. If or the LORD your God goes with you, he will never leave you nor forsake you. Now more than ever we have to embrace our faith."

Kobe bursts out laughing pretending to be holding a female dancing, "The only thing I want to embrace right now is a shorty at the party."

"For real..." Noah rolls his eyes.

He takes his phone from the dashboard and unlocks it. He looks at it momentarily then places it back, "Still waiting on the text. Dre, what else you got for me on that mixtape."

Dre smiles, "There's Drake and..."

"I love that 6 vibe he brings. The guy has got great flow," Noah says.

Kobe starts, "Yeah! I agree but..."

"But what?" Dre interrupts. "You seriously know nothing about mixtapes so just lay off."

Carlos winces in mock pain, "Ouch! Kobe has been hit square in the face."

"Whatever!" Kobe hisses. "Who cares for a blunt?"

Carlos shakes his head, "Not me. I'd rather die with a bottle than with a blunt."

Noah, suddenly uptight, grunts, "No one is dying here man."

"Of course, no one is. Chill bro," Carlos mutters.

Noah reaches for the blunt, "I need to clear my head."

Dre laughs, "Nothing messes with your head more than blunt Noah. You should know that."

"It clears mine though," Kobe says as he looks at the blunt.

"Where do you even get the stuff?" Carlos says with a frown. "I thought you said you weren't dealing."

Kobe seems uncomfortable as the others turn to fix to their gaze on him, "It's complicated but I don't deal."

"It can't be more complicated than being an aspiring black quarterback," Dre adds. "We are listening."

Kobe sighs, "Pops deals."

Dre, Carlos and Noah respond at the same time, "He's in prison."

A moment of silence passes before Carlos asks, "How is that even possible?"

"Anything is possible with Bo Briggs," Kobe scoffs. "I don't know how he does stuff but he always finds a way. So he deals and Reggie gets the dough to me so I can take care of Momma and my siblings."

Carlos is not satisfied, "How did you get this?"

"I don't know..." Kobe shrugs.

"What do you mean you don't know?" Dre demands.

"Well," Kobe says hesitantly, "Reggie sends me on some errands. It's where I get them. Nothing too serious."

Noah shakes his head, "You have to be careful Kobe. The Cops are not smiling so you have got to be careful if you don't want to get into trouble."

"Guys!" Kobe shouts. "You are overreacting. I won't get into trouble. I promise.

Noah checks his phone, "Guys I may get out of here soon. Let's get this party booming."

Carlos suggests, "Or we could just sit and talk about our challenges?"

Dre agrees, "Yeah! Makes a lot of sense."

"So you want us to organise a pity party for ourselves," Noah says, unconvinced.

"Maybe!" Kobe adds. "Or not."

Carlos chimes in, "Not necessarily a pity party. We could help each other ease the burden."

Noah rolls his eyes, "I will just sit here and drink. You guys can go on."

Kobe seems happy to have such a great group of supportive friends, "Alright! Who goes first?"

"Me!" Carlos raises his hand into the air. "It's no news that I am about to join the army..."

Dre laughs, "Which is actually ridiculous to me. Like dude is all brains. He graduated as valedictorian and he wants to go waste away in the army?"

"There are also smart people in the army bro," Noah adds. "Don't make fun of what you don't understand."

Dre retreats, "I ain't making fun of anything. It's the truth. Carlos should be aiming for college, not the army."

Carlos lowers his head, "I wish Pappi would see it that way. It's been so difficult for me. I mean the pressure at home and all."

"I can't claim to understand but I feel your pain," Kobe says as he looks at his friend. "At least your pops is interested in you making the right decisions mine is quite the opposite. My old man anticipates my arrival at the prison. He says there I will know true freedom."

"Your Pappi is unbelievable," Carlos mutters.

"Try mine that wants me a 5 star quarterback to become either a DB or a receiver," Dre points out.

"What the hell!" Noah yells in disbelief. "Wait, what, you're the best quarterback in the state."

"My point exactly," Dre confirms. "But Pops has this strong belief that my best shot to make it the league is not at quarterback."

"The NFL hasn't always been kind to black quarterbacks," Kobe says before adding, "The change is slow and deeply entrenched."

"Still it's not enough reason to want to make him play as a DB," Noah says while deep in thought. "Dre's obviously the best quarterback. Remember the game of last year? Throwing and running, like no other. Six hundred yards passing 200 yards running, come on who does that?"

"I agree too," Carlos adds. "Those stats are crazy."

"Yeah!" Dre nods. "I know and I don't want to but my old man thinks I am doing too much with my Quarterback or nothing stance."

"Meaning?" Kobe asks, confused.

"Obviously he wants Dre to quit being a quarterback. Have you even been listening?" Carlos explains.

"That was a rhetorical question, Carlos," Kobe points out. "It really didn't need an answer. Look who's already acting like a Harvard Stud."

Carlos rolls his eyes at Kobe, "I ain't in yet bro. I may never even get in. Military Stud is more appropriate here."

Noah laughs, "I can't even imagine you in uniform. You are way too soft for that."

"Hello! What do you mean too soft? I consider that an affront on my personality," Carlos seems offended.

Dre chuckles, "He means you don't have the balls to be in the Military and I agree with him."

"Come on guys. That's not fair," Kobe winks at Carlos. "Carlos looks quite capable you know. He has got the face and the body structure."

Carlos smiles and says, "Thank you, Kobe."

"Back to Dre…" Kobe turns his attention to his other friend. "Seriously! Dude, you better stick to your emphatic. You can't listen to your dad, you know. You will regret it."

"I understand that my dad thinks he knows what's best for me but sometimes he doesn't," Dre says as a dark shadow appears under his brow. "He doesn't get it, things have changed."

"Yeah!" Noah agrees. "It's a different story when you are in the game yourself. So what are you going to do?"

"I am so clueless," Dre confirms. "I was considering letting the issue rest for sometime before bringing it up again. Maybe he would be more understanding then."

"What about your mom?" Kobe suggests. "She can talk to him."

Dre shakes his head, "She has and he is still as hard as rock. He thinks she doesn't really understand these things. He says she's my mom and can never understand. It was quite insulting but my mom let it go like she always does his excesses. At a time it seemed he had relented but like they say the leopard can never change its spots no matter how hard he tries."

"Hmm!" Carlos scratches his chin. "It's kinda sad that our parents do not understand us."

"Kobe doesn't need to be understood," Dre says. "He's plain stupid."

"Ouch!" Kobe folds his arms across his chest. "That's harsh man. Cut me some slack. I ain't even doing anything terrible. I am just trying to protect my family."

"By walking in the shoes of your Pops. What a clever decision," Dre accuses.

"That's really sarcastic," Kobe says as he becomes agitated. "I know this may not be the right way to help but I have no choice."

"Oh! No. What you have is plenty of choice. You just chose the easy way out," Carlos pushes.

Kobe, visibly angry, seethes, "All you guys ever do is judge me. I wonder why you judge when you haven't even been through half the stuff I have been through. You both have fathers that are interested in your lives. You have a family that is happy. What do I have? A father in prison, threats every frigging day if I don't help keep the end of his bargain with the gang. I doubt you have had to face the harsh realities of life on your own. I take care of my family but your family takes care of you and you dare judge me for decisions I have made? You have no God damn right."

"I agree with Kobe," Noah says after a few minutes of silence. "Both of you have lesser troubles than we do. A potential Havard Kid and a great quarterback who is soon to play for the NFL. Both of you have it easier. I can't even think of a career because I have too many demons to fight and every day I wake up it gets worse. It's like I am floating and the only way I can see clearly is when I have got a bottle beside me. Each gulp makes my blood heat up. That's the only time I feel alive. When you lose a father and a sister almost at the same time you suddenly begin to lose yourself. It's even worse when you start to lose yourself even before their deaths."

Carlos is taken aback, "Whoa! I am so sorry. I didn't mean to sound judgemental or anything. I was just worried..."

Noah interrupts, "You guys have it way easier. Sometimes I wish I could wake up and see that my life was actually a nightmare then maybe I can start over."

"We are here for you," Dre offers. "We are here to make it easier. That's why we are talking instead of drinking or partying. Yeah! We initially wanted to party but sometimes we have got to sit, talk and make things bare. You can talk to us, Noah."

Noah sighs, "Thanks Dre but I don't think you guys can take it plus I don't want to burden anybody. You guys have the stuff to deal with."

"But we will listen. Don't hide anything from us," Dre adds.

Realizing the full impact of Noah's problem, Carlos nods, "Yeah! Be real with us, Noah. We know you are introverted. You talk to yourself than you talk to people but we can help if you open up. A problem shared is always easier to bear."

"It is, bro," Kobe agrees. "It certainly is. Come on we are listening. We have all had our turns. Now it's your turn."

Noah gulps emotionally and tries to control the tears threatening to spill, "Thanks, guys but I don't think I can. I have never told anybody. I think I will just have to take it to my grave."

"That we won't allow," Carlos reassures his friend. "Spill, Noah. What is it?"

Noah's voice breaks, "I get angrier by the day. I seriously wish things were different. Growing up was fun and awesome. I had a beautiful family until my uncle showed up. The bastard ruined my life. He ruined me."

"How do you mean?" Dre frowns.

"I was abused consistently by my uncle..." Noah states.

"Jeez!" Dre gasps. "The vermin!"

"I knew he was no good but I didn't think he was this horrible. We are truly in perilous times. The end is truly near," Carlos says.

Dre says with sincerity, "I am so sorry, man. I don't even know what to say."

Finding his confidence to speak up, Noah continues, "I hid it for years. I didn't know who to tell and how to because my uncle was a dangerous man and once or twice he had threatened me. I retreated into myself and the only escape I had was alcohol. With alcohol everything was fine. I would drown in bottles after bottles but the next morning the pain would be so raw and the only thing I could do to deaden it was to find pleasure in women. One girl after another till I couldn't even stop myself anymore. My dad watched as I grew worse. He reached out, he wanted to help but he didn't know how because I wasn't talking. Funny he didn't write me off. The time I gathered the strength to tell him was the time fate knew it would strike a fatal blow. Dad was gone and my confession was still bottled up inside me. The cruelest of all is that the bastard died with my father. I felt cheated. He couldn't just go without suffering for his sins. How dare he? I also blame him for my father's death till date."

Dre spits, "He was an expert at dragging people down with him. A horrible piece of shit."

"After Dad died," Noah continues, "My family was torn apart. We were all doing our own thing. Mom became an alcoholic, my sister became totally different. I couldn't help any because I was fighting my own demons. I watched as life sucked them dry. Months later..."

"Your sister committed suicide and it dealt you a devastating blow," Kobe whispers.

"Oh! My!" Carlos cannot believe the amount of emotional trauma his friend has to bear.

Dre shakes his head, "Jeez! What kind of friends are we? We knew you were having a hard time but we had no idea it was this hard. I am so sorry Noah. I wish..."

"No wishes guys," Noah shakes his head. "You weren't at fault. I wanted to deal with it alone."

"We are really sorry," Kobe adds. "Really!"

"From now on, you won't have to suffer alone," Carlos says, "We are here for you. We are your family."

Noah is visibly crying, "Thank you so much guys. I feel better. Much better. Thank you."

Carlos winks, "There are friends that stick closer than brothers. We are those kinda friends."

"We sure are," Dre agrees.

Kobe pats his friend on the back, "We will help each other through the hard times."

"And the good times too, bro," Dre responds. "Don't forget that."

Noah looks towards the dashboard as his phone beeps. He wipes his face and reads the message aloud, "Hi! Come get your mom she's dead drunk."

While his friends stare at him in silence, Noah continues, "Yeah! I got to go."

"How about we go with you?" Carlos offers. "Make sure she's alright and leave after."

"Sounds like a plan," Kobe agrees.

"Alright! Let's go," Noah sighs as he starts the car.

"So much for Champions night out," Dre laughs.

"Not to talk of the juice, blunt and mixtape," Carlos adds.

Kobe smiles, "Timing bro... The timing was should I say not quite right."

"There are other days to celebrate," Noah says in a serious tone, "Champions will always be Champions."

CHAPTER 11

"Is this the time you were expected home?" Otis booms as he watches his son trying to sneak back into the house without waking his parents. "We pleaded with you to come back early but you don't listen. We heard in the news about the gunshots downtown."

Dre stops in his tracks, "We didn't go to a club. We went..."

"I don't care where the hell you went to," Otis booms, "You disobeyed me is the issue I am addressing."

"Come on Pops!" Dre sighs. "I really didn't disobey. It's not like I am coming up in the dead of the night. The night is still young."

Otis draws closer and inhales the smell of alcohol and blunt, "What's that I smell? You been drinking uhn?"

"I just took two swigs," Dre confesses. "I am not even drunk."

"What do you mean, two swigs?" Otis frowns. "Have you ever seen me drinking? Am I not a perfect enough example for you?"

"Uhn!" Dre scoffs. "I have seen you drinking beer especially with your guys..."

"Dre Banks," Otis points a finger at his son, "Shut the hell up before I smack sense into your black head."

"Yes Sir," Dre says sarcastically. "Can I go now?"

"You know what?" Otis continues, ignoring his son. "You are grounded for one week."

"What the hell!" Dre pleads. "You can't do that, Pops. I am supposed to be preparing for the next big game. You can't do this."

"Oh!" Otis snaps furiously. "I damn right can. Plus you can't play if you are not going to play as a DB or receiver. For now, you have to get your head straight."

"This is unbelievable, Pops. You can't do this. It ain't fair," Dre yells as he stomps towards his room.

"Welcome to the real words son. Life isn't fair most of the time," Otis says as he turns his back.

***

Still thinking about their eventful night out, Carlos opens the door to his home.

Seconds later, Sofia sticks her head around the corner and gestures for Carlos to take a seat at the kitchen table, "You didn't tell us you would be coming back this late."

Carlos slops down onto a chair and looks at the plate of food Sofia places in front of him.

"Because I didn't think I would stay out so late," Carlos responds while picking at his food.

"How are the boys?" She asks.

"They are fine just a little down here and there," Carlos lies. "There's nothing we can't fix."

"You aren't eating," Sofia remarks. "You don't like the food, do you?"

"I do," Carlos sighs. "I just that I have a lot on my mind."

"Mind sharing?" Sofia asks.

"Never mind. I'll be fine," Carlos gets up to go to his room.

"Made a decision yet?" Sofia asks.

"Uhm!" Carlos tries avoiding the question. "Don't want to talk about it now. I feel really tired."

***

"You can't keep doing this ma. You have to stop," Noah says as he walks towards his mother.

He had not been home for two minutes and he could already smell alcohol drench the walls.

Nancy smiles and with a slur as a result of the alcohol she has taken, says, "Son, you worry too much. I am perfectly fine. There's nothing wrong with me. I swear there's nothing wrong with me."

"Doesn't seem like it, Ma. You are sick," Noah adds.

"Come on!" Nancy laughs. "I am as healthy as a fiddle. You should try racing me. I would beat you to it."

"I bet you would also be alongside some bottles to make you steady on your feet," Noah responds sarcastically.

"I am happier with the bottles," Nancy sighs. "There's nothing to live for but with the bottles I always find a reason to wake up."

"Am I not enough reason?" Noah seethes. "Am I not good enough to make you want to stay clean?"

"Oh! Son I..." Nancy knows she had gone too far.

"I have watched you waste away on bottles," Noah pleads. "I have watched you drown in them. At first I thought it would make you better but I see everyday how it has torn you apart. See how you look, Ma."

"As beautiful as ever, Son," Nancy smiles. "I feel alive."

Noah hits the table in anger, "You are not alive, Ma. You are slowly disappearing. You need help. You are an alcoholic."

As Noah turns to leave the room, Nancy yells, "Hey! Don't you dare judge me! You are equally as guilty as I am. You think I don't see you but I do. When you hide in the attic drinking yourself to stupor and crying like a baby. You are supposed to be a man but you are not even half the man your uncle was let alone your father."

Noah is seething and bangs the table again. "Damn!" he yells as he throws a bottle against the wall. "How dare you say that? How dare you say that? You are supposed to be the mother here. You are supposed to be the one looking out for your kids. Instead, you turn the other way and pretend everything is fine when things are not. You never saw my pain, my struggles, you never saw me. Damn!"

Nancy's voice breaks, "You can't blame me, Noah. You know you can't blame me. If your dad hadn't followed you to the game maybe he wouldn't have gotten into a ghastly motor accident that killed him."

Noah can't believe his ears, "You blame me."

"Damn right!" Nancy slurs. "I do. I blame you for everything Noah that's why you are not reason enough to stop me from drinking."

"Whoa!" Noah whispers as tears roll down his cheeks. "This is just crazy. Are you even a mother? Are you even human? I would want to believe it's the alcohol talking but the pain is too real to blame on the alcohol. I was broken before but you..."

Noah walks out once more.

"Come back here!" Nancy screams. "Where are you going? I need my bottle, Noah! Give me my bottle!"

***

"Kobe, where you been?" Toni asks as her son returns home.

"Aw!" Kobe smiles. "Ma you worry too much. I am back now so everything is fine."

"Nothing is fine. Nothing is fine. Did you hear the news?" Toni asks.

"What news, Ma?" Kobe frowns.

"There were gunshots reported downtown," Toni whispers. "I get worried everytime you leave the house."

"Didn't hear that," Kobe sighs. "I was nowhere near that stuff. Ma, you are getting paranoid."

"Yes, I am and good reason too," Toni says sternly.

"We have talked about this, Ma," Kobe mumbles. "All I need is a plan."

"The only plan that makes sense here is reporting to the Police," Toni says matter-of-factly.

"The Police?" Kobe shakes his head. "You think that would help? I will end up in jail just like Pops and that's what he wants. I can't end up like Pops. I have great dreams. I have great plans. I can't tell the cops it will only make it worse. What if Reggie and the gang come after you and the kids? I can't risk it."

"Right now I don't care," Toni demands. "All I want is for those thugs to end up in jail and rot there for all I care."

"Even if they are sent to jail, they have connections. They will be out in a week or two. They are smarter than the system."

Toni sighs, "I have a really bad feeling about this, Kobe. I feel so uneasy. Something tells me the end is coming."

"You worry too much," Kobe reassures. "Don't worry I got this."

CHAPTER 12

Kobe is in an alley with a group of young men as well as Reggie.

"Kobe," Reggie says, "It seems like your Pops wants you more involved in the deals. He says it's been difficult for him in there."

"That wasn't the plan Reggie and you know it," Kobe shakes his head.

"Here, plans are subject to change," Reggie warns.

"Damn that man," Kobe fumes. "So what do you want me to do?"

"Simple," Reggie instructs. "You are gonna be making deliveries personally and also be the middleman in our deals. That's the least you can do."

"What if I say no?" Kobe tries.

Reggie takes a gun from his belt and cocks it, "You never know what this can do until it releases a bullet. When it does, it won't be me though. Technically it would be you."

"What does that even mean?" Kobe looks at the gun.

"Let's just say accidents happen," Reggie teases.

"The fact that you threaten me is annoying. You think I am afraid of you but I am not," Kobe adds.

Reggie responds in a serious tone, "You should be if you ever want to have a shot at going to college, you know."

"Shit!" Kobe spits. "This is just shit. I ain't doing this anymore. What if the cops catch me? My life will be ruined then."

"As it stands," Reggie says, "The Cops should be the least of your concerns. This gang is much more dangerous than the Cops, if you understand what I mean."

"You can't force me," Kobe stands his ground. "I could call the Cops on you."

Reggie laughs sarcastically, "And get implicated. Well, if you haven't noticed big bro Young Marley has had a eye for the street. She comes around once or twice but because I respect the effort you put in I let her go."

"The day you lay your hands on my sister is the day you die. The day you..." Kobe is boiling over with anger.

"Just get the job done and your family is safe," Reggie cuts in. "Do you understand?"

"Yeah!" Kobe mutters under his breath. "I gotta go. Meeting my friends for a drink."

"You be a good boy, now..." Reggie taunts as he watches Kobe walk away.

Within the next hour, Kobe is swirling a drink at the far end of a bar, "Why isn't Noah here?" he asks worriedly.

"He called to cancel," Dre says. "His mom is drunk again. He has to take care of her."

"Poor thing!" Carlos shakes his head.

"Yeah! I really feel for him though," Dre adds.

"I suggest he gets therapy," Carlos suggests. "Him and his mom."

"I doubt he would even consider it," Kobe shrugs. "The thing with Noah is that he loves fighting his battles alone."

"As do you," Dre points towards his friend.

"Mine is different," Kobe reasons. "I can't get you all involved in my mess. If I am to go down I want to do it alone."

"Nobody is going down, dude," Carlos adds. "We'll figure this out."

"Thought of a plan yet?" Dre asks, hopeful.

"None yet," Kobe responds. "I am still blank. I am now deep in the game. My Pops dug me into deeper shit. I don't know how I can possibly extricate myself from this mess."

"I thought you said you were going to stop," Carlos frowns.

"Yeah! But it's impossible now. Reggie threatened me," Kobe adds.

"Threatened with what?" Carlos asks.

"With Young Marley," Kobe sighs.

"Shit!" Dre spits. "Dude is a demon."

"Like the hell!" Carlos agrees.

Kobe takes a gulp of his drink, "I don't know what to do man. I seriously think this is the end of me. If I survive this, I... "

"You will survive this," Carlos cuts in. "You got us, bro."

Kobe's phone rings and he picks it up.

"I have got to go now," Kobe says as he puts the phone back into his pocket. "I got some delivery to make. I can't delay. I can't give Reggie any reason to think I am not in. See you around."

"Be careful," Dre pleads.

"I will," Kobe promises before he leaves.

"Well, I need to meet Selena, anyway," Carlos says as he leaves Dre at the bar.

As soon as Carlos gets home, he finds Selena already waiting for him.

"I have missed you, babe," Selena greets him. "I can't believe we haven't seen in like two weeks."

"Yeah!" Carlos smiles. "You've been too busy for me."

"That's not even possible you know," Selena laughs.

"I don't know," Carlos replies as he pecks her on the cheek. "What have you been up to?"

"Nothing much," Selena sighs. "I couldn't get into Havard so I am trying out other schools. I am not as smart as you."

"You are kidding," Carlos responds. "You are smart and you know that. I have learnt so much from you and I am still learning you know."

"Aw! You are such a sweetie," Selena teases.

"Remind me why you feel in love with me," Carlos laughs.

"Look who's high on praise!" Selena adds.

Carlos chuckles, "I am not. I am just happy to have you here with me."

"Me too, babe," Selena says as she snuggles against Carlos.

"Selena," Santiago says as he enters the room, "Have you spoken with Carlos. He's giving me such a hard time. He's rarely ever at home these days running of with his gang."

"They are just my friends, Pappi," Carlos protests.

"Sounds like the same thing to me," Santiago shrugs. "That Kobe kid I don't want you hanging out with him. His family is so much trouble."

"You mean his dad," Carlos says.

"Whatever! Just stop hanging out with him. He's bad news," Santiago warns.

"He's my friend and we are on the same team. I can't do that," Carlos frowns.

"When you finally get into the army your youthful exuberance will cease," Santiago states. "It's a certainty."

"I ain't quitting the team though," Carlos claims.

"Say what?" Santiago cups his hand behind his ear.

"Nothing... He was talking to me," Selena tries to save the situation.

"Alright!" Santiago relaxes once more. "I'll leave you two to it then."

Selena ensures that Santiago is out of earshot before she talks, "Seems you and your dad are still on a fighting spree."

"He's spoiling for a fight but I won't give him the satisfaction," Carlos responds. "I really don't want to drop my dreams of going to college. I don't even want to be in the army. It's just too much for me. He also talks about me having to quit the game. That's not gonna happen."

"Have you made a decision yet?" Selena asks.

Carlos shrugs, "I guess I just have to do what he says if I wanna have peace."

"Wow!" Selena gushes. "Just for peace, you would do anything even to abandon your dreams."

"That seems like the most rational thing to do besides there are more opportunities for me in the army. I could give you a better life, you know."

Selena looks into her boyfriend's eyes, "Carlos, just do whatever your heart says to do. It's not like I am planning to be fully dependent on you. I have my dreams too and I am going to pursue them irrespective of what anybody says. You should too. It's your life plus I won't want to spend the rest of my life with a man that answers to his father. You have got to be a man. Make your choices and bear whatever consequences your choices bring. That's how to be a man, Carlos."

"You amaze me every time," Carlos muses. "How can you be this smart and driven?"

Selena smiles, "You could ask google…"

"Food is ready, guys," Sofia calls. "Come eat."

"Sure! We will join you soon," Selena smiles.

"You know what's more delicious than mom's meal now?" Carlos asks.

"No! What?" Selena responds.

Carlos winks at her as he gets up, "You!"

CHAPTER 13

Young Marley sneaks into the house as Kobe sits outside with his legs stretched out in front of him.

"Hey!" Kobe calls as he sees Marley. "Where are you coming from, young lady?"

Marley stammers, "Uhm... Had to stay late because of extra lessons and uhm..."

"Extra lessons?" Kobe asks. "Who's gonna pay for them?"

"Emm... You?" Marley asks.

Kobe laughs sarcastically, "You think you smart. That's the funny thing. Who knows about the extra classes? Does momma know? Does Zoey know?"

"Uhmm..." Marley does not know what to say.

Kobe calls, "Zoey! Zoey!"

"What?" Zoey shuffles towards the commotion.

"Yeah!" Kobe starts. "Marley says she's coming from extra lessons at school. How true is that?"

"Uhmm!" Zoey looks at Marley. "I can't really tell. She's been coming late these days so I figured she may be really busy at school."

"I stay late because I am busy at school," Marley stares daggers at Zoey.

Zoey rolls her eyes, "If you say so... But one of the neighbors said you've been hanging out with the wrong crowd. I don't even know what that means. Just be careful."

"Mind your business, kiddo," Marley barks at Zoey.

Zoey frowns, "I don't see why you are mad at me. I am just concerned..."

"Keep your frigging concern to..." Marley continues.

"Shut up!" Kobe cuts in. "Just shut your mouth, Marley. What's wrong with you?"

"Nothing!" Marley mutters.

"Do you even pity Momma?" Kobe asks. "She's going through a lot. We all are going through a lot. You should be more careful."

"I don't see what I am doing wrong," Marley adds. "You are always quick to judge me, Kobe. You never cut me slack. You are way easier on Zoey than you are on me."

"What?" Kobe asks, confused.

"Yeah!" Marley continues. "I feel suffocated every day in this house. This house is always glommy with everybody looking sullen. It was way better when pops was around."

Kobe is wide-eyed, "Pops again! Kiddo doesn't even know what he has done to us. The problem with you, Marley, is that you think you know when actually you really don't know any frigging thing."

"I don't believe you," Marley adds. "Reggie told me Pops is doing fine and may soon be released. He…"

"Reggie what?" Kobe and Zoey say at the same time.

"Marley," Zoey starts, "That dude is dangerous. Why the hell did you get mixed up with him?"

"He isn't though," Marley says while trying to act mature. "I had to know something. He is the only friend Pops has."

"He landed Pops into shit," Zoey responds. "You know that, we all know that. Marley, you are screwing up."

Kobe is exasperated, "So Reggie has been the one taking you extra lessons uhn? So what did he tell you? That Pops is a hero of some sort and you should be proud of him? How Pops is a good father and he gave himself up for his family? That's the bullshit he been telling you?"

"Yeah! And it ain't bullshit," Marley protests.

Kobe runs his hands over his face, "I feel like wriggling your tiny neck. How can you be so stupid? Fraternizing with the enemy."

"I thought you are the older and smarter one but apparently, it doesn't work that way. I know to avoid Reggie how come you don't," Zoey adds.

Marley snarls, "Because unlike you, I don't write people off."

Kobe claps sarcastically, "Oh! Wow! You suddenly are a saint. You don't even know the kind of devil you are dealing with."

"Reggie is not a devil, why can't you see it?" Marley defends.

"There's nothing to see there," Kobe scoffs. "You are just blinded by... Wait, do you like Reggie?"

"That's ridiculous," Marley laughs. "Reggie is way older than me and even if I admire his person we would never work."

Toni enters, oblivious to what's happening, "Who are you admiring, honey?"

Kobe and Zoey both yell, "Reggie!"

Toni stops dead in her tracks, "He who is not to be named? That's who you are admiring. That's a mistake right, you don't mean it."

"I have just been hanging out with Reggie, Ma. Nothing more," Marley starts.

"You what?" Toni is visibly shocked. "What the hell!"

Kobe spits, "She's just a spoilt child who doesn't know her left from right. What have you been doing hanging out with Reggie?"

"Well, nothing much..." Marley tries to defend herself.

"What do you mean nothing much?" Toni screams. "Spit it out girl before I knock the life outta you!"

Marley begins to shake, "I just told him I wanted to see Pops."

"Seeing your dad would be the least of your worries by the time I..." Toni raises her hand to slap Marley but is restrained by Kobe.

"No!" Kobe pleads. "Ma, don't. Let me see your bag, Marley."

Marley shifts from one foot to another, "Why? There's nothing in my bag just books."

"Give it to me!" Kobe demands.

"You heard your bro," Toni adds. "Give him the damn bag."

Kobe snatches the bag from Marley picks the book out, "If you have been hanging out with Reggie then there's no way you would be clean. There's stuff."

Some wraps fall out and Zoey gasps, "Jeez! You been dealing."

"I swear I haven't," Marley weeps.

"You been dealing Marley. Gosh! You been dealing. How did I not see it?" Kobe shouts.

Toni, exasperated, adds, "How did I not? This is crazy. Marley's been dealing under my roof and I didn't even know."

"It's all my fault. It's all my fault. Reggie, that bastard," Kobe repeats.

"What the hell is wrong with all of you?" Toni yells. "Haven't we suffered enough? Haven't we? Why are we hell bent on doing more damage than your father already did?"

"Pops did no damage. He was..." Marley tries.

"He was what?" Kobe scoffs. "Just shut your mouth."

"This is the problem!" Marley states. "Everyone shuts me up. You never listen to me but Reggie does."

"What else you been doing with Reggie? Has he ever touched you?" Kobe demands.

Marley screams, "No! We just talk."

Toni tries to control her agitation, "Go to your room, Marley. You are grounded."

"You can't do that, Ma!" Marley wails.

"Yes I can," Toni responds. "Now go to your room before you receive some more punishment for your poor choices."

Marley stomps towards her room with Zoey in tow.

Toni looks back at Kobe, "This is all your fault, Kobe. I blame you for this."

Kobe sighs, "I think Reggie involved Marley because I threatened to leave. He threatened me some days earlier with Marley. I didn't know..."

"You didn't know what?" Toni asks. "You didn't know Reggie is a devil and he can do unimaginable evil? There's no excuse for this Kobe. This is getting out of hand. I can't have my kids involved in this kind of thing. It's dangerous as hell."

"I know, Ma. I know..."

"How are you going to fix this?" Toni pleads. "How are we going to fix this?"

"I really wish I knew," Kobe responds. "I have been thinking still nothing is coming. Reggie is dangerous and with the number of threats he has issued to me I am kinda scared of double-crossing him. What if he hurts you or the girls?"

"I really don't care anymore. Reggie has crossed a line by involving Marley. He has crossed a line and nobody is totally invincible. Reggie must go down," Toni punches a fist in the air.

"Yeah!" Kobe agrees. "But when he does I don't want him going with us. Dude is crazy, Ma."

"Dude is crazy but he ain't crazier than a mother trying to protect her kids," Toni states.

"I will handle this, Ma," Kobe promises. "Please don't get yourself involved."

"I have waited too long," Toni ignores her son. "I am tired of living under the shackles Reggie has placed on us."

"I am too and I looking for away. It won't be long, Ma. I promise it won't be long," Kobe says once more.

CHAPTER 14

The guys hang out shooting some hoops, enjoying some time away from their troubles.

Dre is smiling, "Good news guys."

"Tell us," Carlos responds.

"Had a long talk with my dad and as it stands you've got yourself a black quarterback going all the way to NFL," Dre says proudly.

"This is great news, man," Kobe adds. "We need some juice for this."

"Emm... No juice please. The last time I got sick as hell," Carlos sighs.

"As did I," Dre adds.

"Mom is currently getting therapy to help with her drinking. She's really doing well. We both have found a reason to do better and be better," Noah tells his friends.

"Told her about your uncle yet?" Kobe asks.

"Yeah!" Noah keeps his head down. "She was so sad but you know that trauma can't be undone overnight. We are moving past the problems we have made and trying to be better. It isn't easy but it's worth every try."

"Hm! Mine is still simmering though but I finally told Reggie I quit," Kobe announces.

Carlos is wide-eyed, "What did he say?"

"That he was gonna make my life a living hell," Kobe says.

"I think you should just report him to the Police," Noah suggests.

"Yeah!" Kobe agrees. "But I ain't no snitch. Momma threatened to call the cops on him if he ever disturbed me again but we know Reggie is not to be put off by that sort of threat. His gang is deep with thugs. He is somewhat invincible."

"No one is, Kobe," Dre reassures. "I feel his end is near. Have you been listening to the news? The police is are keen to shut the dealers down."

"From reports it's quite serious," Carlos says. "Anyone who gets caught up in that stuff is going to serve some hard time. How old Reggie is if caught, he might to old for this game when he gets out."

Dre laughs,"Yeah! He is old school, though."

"What about Marley?" Noah asks. She cool now?"

"Better than before, still rebellious though but now she has come to terms with the fact that Pops may never come back. He's been causing a lot of trouble in prison and they may have him transferred," Kobe concludes.

"Poor Marley loves her Daddy," Dre adds.

"That sounds dope though. I'll give you that!" Noah says.

Dre laughs, "My lines are always cool you know bro. Always..."

"This is where we call you proud," Kobe responds.

Dre laughs, "A black quarterback has every right to be proud. Ain't nobody prouder right now man."

"Made a decision yet, Carlos?" Kobe asks.

"Um..." Carlos mumbles. "I am actually sticking with College maybe after College I will figure out if to join the army or not. I have my whole life in front of me and wouldn't want to rush anything. I told Pappi and we have come to an understanding."

"Wow!" Kobe gushes. "You guys have found a way forward."

"We all have," Carlos nods, "Reggie should lay off you now because the Cops are on his scent."

"Yeah!" Kobe adds. "He hasn't called in over a week. I hope he never calls though because this time I am truly done."

"Great decision man," Noah pats his friend on the back. "One of the best you've ever made."

"Coach Taylor called some days back," Noah changes the subject. "Wanted to know when I am getting back to the gym."

"What did you tell him?" Dre asks.

"Soon maybe," Noah responds. "I don't want to go in with a messed up head. My come back will be a hit man. I have been out for too long. For now I am focusing on my mental health and..."

"Body health too," Kobe cuts in. "I noticed it's been a while you drank anything except water."

Carlos laughs, "Yeah! Right. Imagine him turning down a bottle of Dom. So unusual but it's cool. Good work Noah."

Noah smiles, "Wouldn't have been possible without your help guys. You stood by me and for that I am forever indebted to you."

"We wish we had come to your rescue sooner, though," Kobe offers. "Maybe things wouldn't have gotten this bad?"

"Every disappointment is a blessing in disguise," Carlos recites. "Every storm has a silver lining, bro. Ain't that what they say?"

Dre scoffs, "You beginning to sound like the old pastor in church with brimming hats, snake-like eyes, and constant hallelujahs."

"Really! I should feel a way but I don't," Carlos laughs.

"You are high on joy right now maybe that's why you aren't mad at Dre. Who knows?" Kobe adds.

Carlos shrugs, "Maybe!"

"Dre, what about the girl?" Noah asks.

"What girl?" Dre responds.

"The girl we been seeing you with?" Noah squints.

"There's no constant man, he's with a different one every day," Kobe laughs.

"Whoa!" Carlos gasps. "That blow was below the belt. Dre! Kobe just called you a player. What you gonna do about that?"

Dre laughs, "Nothing! It's sort of a complement. It's no fault of mine the girls love me. I mean who wouldn't? You guys do too."

"Slow down, bro," Noah laughs. "

"Seriously!" Dre adds. "There's no girl, though. If there was I would have told you. Maybe I would be singing it the way Carlos sings Selena's name on the rooftops."

"Whatever but I love it," Carlos concludes.

"Man's focused on career and big dreams," Dre comments. "The ladies will cause distraction and I am just too tight for that."

"You know you just indirectly meant that I ain't got big dreams because I have a woman," Carlos peruses.

"Carlos!" Dre squeals. "You are being ridiculous."

"I hope Zoey doesn't hear this because she's going to launch a full diatribe on how the society is misogynistic and a whole lot of stuff about feminism and women empowerment. Carlos is acting like Carlos though," Kobe says.

Dre says thoughtfully, "What's that stuff called feminism about anyway? My momma is cool just the way she is. She says it's alot."

"Mine says it's not scriptural," Carlos comments.

"All I know is they are fighting for gentler equality..." Kobe smiles at his own pun.

"Or equity?" Noah adds.

"Nah!" Dre chimes in. "Man. Gender equality not possible but Gender equity maybe we can try."

"Get ready to be called out," Carlos suggests.

"Ouch!" Dre comments. "That's harsh."

"The whole concept about feminism is much needed ," Carlos defends.

"I agree with some of their stuff, though," Kobe mutters.

Dre nods, "Humor me, Carlos."

Carlos shrugs. "They say a lot but I still don't understand the concept. My mama says they are fighting for justice. It's going to be a really long fight but I don't think they will win."

"Why is that?" Dre asks.

"Simple!" Noah begins. "It's a male dominated society and if you don't fit the mold things are tough. The fact is a lot of different people are having a hard time fitting in certain areas..."

"Thank the Lord for Dre," Carlos claps his hands.

Noah holds his hand up, "I admit. I was one hell of a player."

Dre adds animatedly, See who talks in past tense. Your playboys days are really over, bro."

"They really are," Noah agrees.

"Let's get some stuff at Eddie's and then drive around listening to the mixtape?" Carlos asks.

They leave the basketball court, ready to head over to Eddie's Convenience Store.

As they get closer to the shop, Dre pipes up, "I wonder why it's called a convenience store when it's so tight and crowded. You can't even get a drink inside plus the store owner is such an upright fellow."

Noah sighs, "Who wouldn't be uptight in this area. Eddie's been robbed a couple of times but dude keeps going."

Carlos reminds them, "Only three persons are allowed in there. Who's gonna go?"

"I, 2, 3... Noah, stay with the car," Dre says.

Noah rolls his eyes, "Always with the car. Do your thing, though." He throws some cash to Dre, "Drinks on me, boys."

"Uhm! Alcohol?" Carlos asks.

"Yeah! Why not?" Noah responds.

"I thought you said…" Kobe starts.

"I didn't say I was completely done," Noah adds. "I said I was a work in progress and I wouldn't want to miss out on this with my guys."

Carlos whispers to Dre and Kobe, "Should we? He is going sober."

Noah frowns, "I can hear you."

Carlos mutters, "No offense. Just looking out for you.

"Alright!" Noah sighs. "Get me any other juice. Someone needs to be sober on our way home. I am being the better man here."

Dre smiles, "We appreciate, man."

As they enter the store, the store owner looks at them with a grumpy expression on his face, "What do you want?"

"Dude..." Dre begins.

"Just get what you want and let's get out," Carlos cuts in.

Kobe looks at the store owner, "Drinks! We want drinks."

The store owner frowns while getting the drinks, "Here!"

Kobe whispers something into Carlos' ear and they both laugh, "Dre! You know..."

The store owner continues, "You guys are always so loud. Sh! Keep it low would you?"

Dre frowns, "You are always tweeking when we come in here. I wish I didn't have to come here."

The store owner stretches his hand, "Give me my money."

Carlos, irritated, answers, "Sure! We aren't thugs."

The store owner growls, "Doesn't look like that to me though."

As they leave the store, Dre is fuming, "The dude is so annoying. He has so much attitude."

"He is probably unhappy with his life you know. You never can tell," Carlos suggests.

"Still no excuse to rub it on me," Dre shrugs.

"You mean us," Kobe corrects. "Funny enough he smiles with other customers. He's always grumpy when it's our turn."

"Maybe he's jealous of good-looking brothers," Dre says.

Carlos laughs, "Yeah! Right."

As they get to the car, Noah yells, "Feels like I have been waiting for eternity. What took you so long?"

"The store owner is a frigging Grinch," Dre laughs.

"Delayed?" Noah asks.

"Delayed and complained," Kobe says. I felt like I was suffocating in there with his stare and all. I am glad I am breathing fresh air now."

"Fresh air free from hate," Dre adds. "I have got to do something to piss him off."

"What?" Carlos frowns.

Dre climbs into the car and honks the horn so loud, the boys laugh and they drive off blaring loud music, drinking and having a great time.

Dre, now slightly drunk, looks at Noah, "Noah, go faster. Why did you slow down?"

"To be safe," Noah responds.

"Ain't no reason to drive like a bitch," Dre complains.

"Whoa!" Kobe and Carlos adds. "Chill, man."

Carlos repeats, "Ain't no reason to drive like a bitch."

Noah slows down as he sees approaching headlights, "Shit! Shit!"

Carlos is drowsy, "What that?"

"Are those cops I see?" Kobe asks.

"They are," Noah mutters.

"Gentlemen. Slow down now and stop the car," a cop announces over the loudspeaker.

Kobe is suddenly alert, "What are we gonna do now?"

"Are we all clean?" Noah asks.

"Yeah!" Carlos confirms. "Just a little tipsy from the juice."

Dre adds with a hiccup, "They got nothing on us, bro, except the alcohol."

Noah sighs, "Which is still an offence aside the loud music. Kobe, you clean?"

Kobe yawns, "Yeah! I… Shit! Shit!"

Noah stops the car and puts off the speaker while the Cops approach, "You clean Kobe?" He asks again.

Kobe's voice breaks, "Shit! I got some blunt in my pocket."

"The hell!" Carlos growls. "I thought you said you ain't trapping."

"Jeez!" Noah shuts his eyes.

"Step out of the car with your hands raised above your head. It's an order," the cop commands.

Kobe is jittery, "What am I gonna do now? What am I...?"

"Just shut up and act cool," Noah whispers.

"We are done for. Damn!" Dre complains.

Carlos growls, "How did the blunt get into your pocket if you were done dealing? This is just stupid. We will all go to jail for this."

Noah keeps his voice down, "Nobody is going to jail."

"Step out of the car now," the cop commands again. "Slowly, gentlemen."

Kobe is shivering, "My bad guys. I didn't mean for this to happen I swear."

"It was really stupid of us to go drinking and driving this late in the night," Noah adds.

The cop questions Dre, "What are you doing by this time of the night blaring speakers like that?"

Dre answers with a slur, "I know my right officer. I know my..." Before he can contain himself, he throws up.

The cop moves back, "Oh! You guys been drinking?"

"I am their driver, officer and I am sober," Noah says with confidence.

"Sober uhn?" the cop scoffs. "Doesn't seem like any of you are."

Carlos gives another hiccup, "But we are."

"I have to run a check on you all . You seem quite intoxicated to me," the cop continues.

"That isn't necessary off..." Kobe says with his head bowed.

"A drunk dude teaching me how to do my job," the cop says sarcastically.

He starts his search at Noah and then moves over to Dre.

"You both clean," the cop confirms.

The cop then searches Carlos and moves over to Kobe.

"You got a flu? Why are you shivering like that?" the cop asks as he sees Kobe shivering.

"Uhm! No... Yes..." Kobe stammers.

"What's this I feel?" the cop asks as his hand moves over Kobe's blunt.

"Don't know," Kobe replies.

"It's deep in your coat and it's wrapped. I think I got something," the cop says as he pulls the parcel wrapped tightly.

"Shit!" Dre says as he throws up again.

Kobe is frantic, "I don't know what that is, I swear."

"Let's find out," the cop says.

He slowly unwraps the parcel as the rest watch in dread.

The cop's eyes light up as he begins to laugh, "Whoa! Dude, you do mixtapes? This is Lil Wayne no ceilings from as far back as 2009! You kidding?"

Caros hiccups and whispers under his breath, "Saved by the Mixtape."

Dre chuckles, Saved by the Mixtape, you mean."

Kobe almost faints from anticipation but suddenly regains his composure, "Emm... Yeah... Emm..."

Noah heaves a sigh of relief as Dre collapses, vomiting again.

CHAPTER 15

Selena is seen sitting on a porch eating some grapes while gently rubbing her pregnant belly.

Carlos opens the front door and sees her, "Hey! Baby, I didn't know you were out here. I thought you were in the room."

"Yeah! I just thought to come out here. The air is fresh and I just wanted to enjoy the scenery," Selena smiles.

Carlos sits and holds her hand, "How are you feeling?"

Selena laughs, "Heavy as ever, Darling. Can't wait to get this baby out."

"I am also excited but you have to wait for the good of us all," Carlos exclaims.

"Of course!" Selena reassures.

"I can't believe how fast time flies," Carlos sighs, "Some years back we were only teenagers in love. Now we are soon to be parents. It's just amazing and unbelievable at the same time."

"Tell me about it," Selena rolls her eyes. "It just brings to mind how that life is in phases and..."

"And men in sizes," Carlos adds. "That cliché hasn't sounded any better."

"I know right," Selena agrees. "Well, in a couple of months we will have our little one running around."

"My little Carlos," Carlos says dreamily.

"I thought we talked about this," Selena frowns. "We are calling him Jordan and not Carlos if it's a boy. What's with you and that Carlos name, though?"

"I don't know. I just love the name. If it's a girl?" Carlos changes the subject.

"I love it too but I want to hear something different. A girl? Never really thought about it," Selena confesses.

"You are tired of me already. That's not fair," Carlos laughs.

Selena leans over to give Carlos a hug, "Not yet and I don't think I will be for a very time."

"You make me blush every single time. I love you, Babe, and our little one," Carlos says lovingly.

"Oops! He or she just kicked. I guess he or she's saying he or she loves you too," Selena puts her hand over her belly.

Carlos laughs as he leans and puts his ear on Selena's belly, "Hey little one! It's your Papa. I can't wait for you to come out of Mama's belly. I really don't know why you don't want us to know the sex of the baby."

"He or she kicked again," Selena whispers. "I don't know but I want the birth to be a surprise. We love you Carlos and I have no doubt you will make a great father.

"You will make an awesome Mama, Darling," Carlos says as he kisses Selena.

***

Dre is on the phone with his mother, "Hi Momma!"

"Hello! Dre, how're you holding up?" Cheryl asks from the other side of the line.

"So far so good, Momma. I am doing quite well. How is Pops?" Dre says.

"Well, you know your Pops. He hasn't ceased complaining but with time he will get used to your absence," Cheryl sighs.

Dre scoffs, "You mean he will get used to my choice. My absence is not the issue Momma and you know it. I am really glad that I stuck with my choice. It's really been amazing."

"You're the only black quarterback, yeah?" Cheryl asks.

"Yeah!" Dre replies. "Momma, but it makes no difference here. I am treated great and they recognize and appreciate my talent."

"I am glad to hear that," Cheryl smiles. "What about classes? How have they been?"

"Classes have been great too," Dre murmurs. "Political science is a really interesting discipline. Asides the constant arguments between students on different issues it's actually amazing to see the depth of the human mind. You know our lecturer was telling us about..."

Cheryl interrupts her son, "When are we expecting you home?"

"Uhm... Don't know, Mom," Dre sighs.

"How about this weekend?" Cheryl suggests.

"I don't think so, Momma, but I will call and whenever I get the chance I will come home," Dre says.

"For a while there I thought you were starting to avoid me and your Pops," Cheryl says jokingly.

"You? No! Pops? Maybe," Dre confesses.

"Come off it, baby. Just give him time," Cheryl pleads.

"I am not waiting around for his approval anymore. I am happy where I am," Dre says matter-of-factly.

"Where is that?" Cheryl asks.

"Right here doing what I love to do," Dre reassures.

"All right, baby. I have got to now. Stay safe for Momma," Cheryl greets.

"I will, though for me mostly," Dre jokes.

***

Noah looks at his mother sitting across from him in the living room, "Hey! Mom, have you taken your medication? You aren't supposed to miss any."

"Oh! I haven't, though," Nancy closes her eyes.

"Let me get them for you. You should be consistent with these things," Noah says as he returns with a couple of labeled bottles.

"Thank you, Noah," Nancy says sincerely. "I wonder what I would do without you."

"We are here for each other mom. We have each other's back. We are all we have," Noah opens the bottles and takes a pill from each.

Nancy swallows as she says, "Thank you, son."

"I am here for you, Mom; whatever you need," Noah confirms.

"Aren't you working today?" Nancy asks.

"Oh!" Noah nods, "I will. I just wanted to relax and spend some time with you. I would be out in an hour or two."

"How's work?" Nancy tries making small talk.

"It's okay. At least we have something to get by every day," Noah smiles.

"Yeah!" Nancy agrees. "As soon as I am better I would get a job."

Noah shakes his head in approval, "Let's get you well first."

"Yes, of course," Nancy looks down at her shoes, "I am better now. I am changed."

"You bet," Noah kisses his mom and rushes out.

***

Kobe squirms as he sits across from his father in the prison visiting room. Bo looks at his son proudly but cannot help feeling emotional.

"Hey!" Kobe greets. "Pops, I am glad to see you are doing all right. It's been quite a while and I am sorry I couldn't come earlier, I had to fix some things."

"No problem, Son. You look great, though," Bo adds.

Kobe smiles shyly, "Well, let's just say Momma has been doing her best."

"And the girl too," Bo says.

Kobe is curious, "What girl?"

Bo, with a mischievous grin on his face, adds, "Come on son. You young guys these days are making waves in ways we didn't dare. Surely while you were away you had someone to come home to."

"Yeah! That's if you mean my friends," Kobe scoffs.

"So, no girl?" Bo asks again.

"Absolutely no one," Kobe reassures.

"Why is that?" Bo does not let go of the subject. "You are young and full of life, Kobe."

"My life is so chaotic, Pops," Kobe sighs. "Besides, I am not ready for any entanglements. I have to keep a level head. Eyes on the prize pops. You know what I mean."

"Of course, I do, son," Bo beams. "I am happy to see you. This apple grew very far from the tree and your Momma has done a better job raising you than I could ever imagine."

"Thank you, Pops," Kobe adds.

"I know I was never going to be a good model for my kids," Bo confides. "I knew if I wanted a shot at raising my kids right it would be to have a wonderful woman in my life. You are proof I made the right choice, Kobe."

"Oh!" Kobe looks his father in the eyes, "Pops, we acknowledge you have made mistakes but we don't judge you. I did before though. I was particularly mad at the way you lived your life. It was hard pops but I think I have grown and I understand that the choices you made may be wrong but it doesn't make you a horrible person. You were just trying to look out for your family the way you thought was right. You did what you had to do, Pops."

"I knew my choices would have adverse effects on you but still made those choices," Bo sighs, "It was selfish of me, Kobe. I won't let you smooth talk the guilt I feel away. Violence never pays and to think I wanted you behind bars with me makes me sick."

Kobe reaches for his father's hand, "It's all right, Pops. I learned from everything and in the end I made my choice which was the best. Don't blame yourself. We all at one time or the other have done and said things we aren't proud of. The important thing is to learn and move on."

"It's difficult, son," Bo says in a shaky voice, "It's really difficult to look past the hurt I have caused you and your siblings and especially your Momma."

"I have forgiven you, Pops," Kobe confirms. "You should forgive yourself."

"Your Momma hasn't called in a long while and Marley, on her last visit, said it would be her last," Bo lowers his head.

"They will all come around, Pops. Seeing you are a changed man will help them heal," Kobe tries consoling his father.

"I hope so," Bo says. "Being behind bars has drummed some sense into me. Sense I should have had long ago."

"Every opportunity you get to be better is an opportunity," Kobe adds. "You shouldn't beat yourself over it, Pops."

Bo sighs, "Enough of me. How are the boys?"

"So far so good, Pops. Carlos is expecting a baby soon."

"Whoo!" Bo smiles. "That's a big one. With the Selena girl, right?"

"Of course. Carlos had eyes for no other," Kobe confirms.

"And even if he did, he is too principled. He still goes on and on about scripture stuff, right?"

Kobe laughs, "Yeah! His latest is that he wishes we all be saved."

"Carlos has always been a great kid," Bo adds. "Calm and cool. He is in the marines?"

"Yeah! After several back and forth with his pops, his old man finally won."

"But is he happy?" Bo asks.

"I really can't tell," Kobe says truthfully. "He seems happy, though."

"So tell me about college. I want to know. How is it?"

"It's no different from the world outside," Kobe says. "It's almost the same routine except for the lectures. But there are so many people to meet, new stuff to learn both the good and bad if you are adventurous, and new stuff to try."

"Sounds interesting."

"It really is," Kobe nods.

"You really are having the time of your life. I am glad you are."

"Oops! I almost forgot," Kobe gasps.

"What's that? Come on don't leave anything out," Bo asks, ready for a story.

"Emm... I know I told you before there's no girl."

"Yeah!" Bo smiles.

"But there's this girl that has sort of got my heart beating," Kobe confesses.

Bo laughs, "Is she pretty?"

"She's a dime, Pops," Kobe nods. "How could you even ask me that? She's super-duper pretty and smart too. She majors in Fine Arts though so I don't see her quite often."

Kobe smiles shyly, "I feel so self-conscious sometimes. She seems like she's privileged and all."

"That shouldn't stop you," Bo answers. "Ain't nobody ever gonna put you down until you do so yourself. She may be privileged and you are special you own it. You are going places, Kobe. Know that and know peace."

"Damn!" Kobe gasps. "Look who's become a motivational speaker. You got me pumping adrenaline right now, Pops. Let's hope it's sustained when I get to see her again."

"I hope it does," Bo adds.

Kobe checks his watch and Bo says, "You need to go. It's almost time."

"I don't mind waiting till time up," Kobe nods.

"Thanks, Son."

"It's no bother, Pops," Kobe looks at his father with pride.

CHAPTER 16

Kobe, Dre, and Noah are hanging out at a coffee shop for some well-deserved time off.

"What do you guys wanna drink?" Kobe asks.

"I need something soft," Dre smiles. "I am a player, you know."

"You know, that sounds funny," Noah adds.

Kobe laughs, "Right! So what do you play, Dre? Ball or girls?"

"You are crazy, man," Noah laughs.

Dre shakes his head, "Where did I meet you guys? Y'all a bunch of clowns."

"With you being the chief clown," Kobe confirms.

"I don't know what you're talking about," Dre places the order and moments later, they're sipping their drinks.

"Carlos," Kobe points out, "Didn't show up because married men get too serious."

"He is trying to be an example of a good father to his kid," Dre laughs.

"I hear you," Noah agrees.

"Is it a girl or boy?" Kobe asks.

Noah shrugs, "How would I know?"

"You referring to a human as it shocks the daylight outta me," Dre mentions.

Kobe rolls his eyes, "I am right, though. I want a girl."

"What?" Dre says wide-eyed, "No way. I can't hold myself if Carlos starts showing up with a girl looking all pink at our meetings."

"Hmm!" Noah adds. "What's the issue with girls and pink, though?"

"If I knew I wouldn't be here, would I?" Dre laughs.

Noah scoffs, "Where else would you be?"

"That was a rhetorical question, dude," Dre exclaims.

"I know," Noah jokes.

Kobe laughs at his friends, "You two."

"So what's up?" Dre asks. "We are supposed to be catching up. Wow! My lines are dope, though."

"As well as lame, bro," Kobe smiles.

"Guys!" Noah laughs.

"Well, you get my point. Let's shoot," Dre changes the subject.

"Mine has been so far so good," Noah confirms. "AA meetings with Momma are working these days. It's amazing to see how much she's changed. I know we aren't there yet but every day is a step in the right direction.

Dre smiles, "Nice one, bro. But you know you have to really keep a close eye on your Momma."

"I know. She's been clean for months."

"How clean?" Kobe asks.

"Real clean," Noah replies.

"Wow!" Dre gushes. "That's amazing, bro. I am super glad."

"What's next for you, Noah?" Kobe asks. "You plan on driving Lyft for a while, right?"

"Yeah! As soon as we are certified clean I plan on getting my college degree."

"Nice one, bro," Kobe slaps his friend on the back.

"Thanks," Noah says.

"What about ball?" Dre asks.

"For now I am sorta just chilling," Noah sighs, "I may get back, I may not. We'll see."

"That's great, Noah. I am happy for you," Kobe adds.

"Me too, bro," Dre agrees.

Kobe sighs, "For me, life hasn't been easy but we stretch every day."

Noah raises his hands, "Preach, brother."

"I almost thought Carlos had stepped in," Dre says. "With you shouting preach, we just may have Carlos running here for some sermons.

Kobe laughs, "Old Carlos and his sermons. Still in love with the Lord as far as I can remember."

Noah smiles, "With a child about to drop he certainly gotta hold on tighter."

"You bet," Dre laughs.

"Life has been fair enough," Kobe starts, "I gotta see my Pops some days again and I must say it's amazing to see my old man changed."

"Finally, old Bo accepts change," Noah claps his hands.

"This sounds interesting," Dre seems intrigued.

"Oh! It is," Kobe confirms. "I don't know what happened to him there but he has learned his lesson. He kept apologizing."

"Whoa!" Noah exclaims, "That's a big one. Old Bo is set in his ways. He never apologizes."

"I know, but he did. He seemed good with my decisions and kept asking questions about college."

"He never wanted you in College," Noah points out.

"He wanted you with him behind bars. This is a big one," Dre adds.

I know, right. It was really amazing. I can say for once my Pops was genuinely interested in me."

Dre sips his drink, "That's great. I hope he gets out soon so your family can be whole again."

"My family was never whole but it will be a chance to mend it. I really hope he gets out soon."

"Did you tell your Momma?" Noah asks.

"Yeah! But she didn't seem interested. She said he may just be putting up an act. I don't think so. He was repentant and was on the verge of tears. I saw tears threaten to spill guys. I have never seen pops that way before."

Dre looks optimistic, "I hope he gets out soon, Kobe. I hope he does."

"Yeah!" Kobe changes the subject, "What's up with you?"

"Nothing much; just school and sports," Dre says. "I am having the time of my life playing for the team."

"You're still the only black quarterback on the team, right?" Kobe asks.

"Yeah! Coach says I am unique. A once in a lifetime player."

"I can imagine how smug you were," Noah narrows his eyes.

Dre smiles, "You bet."

"Your Pops?" Kobe asks.

"My Momma called some days ago and said he complains now and then but I really don't mind. I am doing what I love and that's the most important thing."

"It is," Noah confirms.

"What about the girls?" Dre asks, "When am I playing a best man again?"

"Uhm! There's a girl," Kobe says.

"There's a what?" Dre is astonished. "Come on, now. Who's she?"

"Emm... Just a girl in class," Kobe blushes.

"Just a girl?" Dre asks. "She's not just a girl, dude."

Noah jokes, "Here I was thinking you were a monk."

"What? You didn't think that, did you?" Dre asks.

"I am sure he didn't. Did you?" Kobe plays along.

Noah laughs, "Come on guys! I was kidding. Have you lost your sense of humor?"

"Uhm! I broke mine," Dre says in mock seriousness.

"Is it a mutual thing?" Noah asks.

"Nah! I doubt she even knows me," Kobe confesses.

"So you got us worked up over a crush?" Dre laughs.

"Dre is actually the most dramatic human I have ever met," Noah adds.

"Well, thank you," Dre says.

"It wasn't a compliment," Noah smiles.

"I consider it a compliment," Dre says again.

"I like her, though," Kobe says dreamily. "There's just something about her."

Dre rolls his eyes, "Oh! Like the way she curves her pen when she writes."

Noah laughs, "Dre, where the heck are you from?"

Kobe scoffs, "I have no idea, bro."

"I am the life of the party, you know," Dre praises himself.

"We appreciate that," Kobe says.

"Sometimes I don't," Noah jokes.

"I love you too," Dre laughs.

"We could try hang at Carlos' next time," Noah suggests.

Dre nods, "Yeah! It's been a while."

"You have to give the soon-to-be daddy a heads up," Kobe adds.

Dre smiles, "Of course, we will. Selena is really homely so I expect a house full of exquisite dishes."

"Besides, we need to know how he is doing," Kobe frowns.

Dre agrees, "Yeah! It's been a while. I wonder how he is faring in the marines."

"Fine, I guess. There's money in the Marines," Noah takes a sip of his drink.

"His father got him a future so secure," Dre adds.

"You think?" Kobe adds. "What about what he wants?"

"He probably realized he wanted it too," Dre suggests.

Noah shakes his head, "Carlos has never been the sort of person that forces things. He was probably tired of fighting with his Pops."

"I guess," Dre shrugs.

“Let's finish up, guys,” Noah suggests. “I have to get
back home.”

CHAPTER 17

Carlos beams as he opens the door to find his friends looking back at him, "Hey, guys!"

Kobe hugs him, "It's been such a long time, bro."

Carlos smiles, "Yeah, it has. I feel so old already."

Noah taps Carlos lightly on the back, "You look good. Selena has been good to you."

Dre winks at Carlos, "I hope you have some beer?"

"Like you don't know Carlos is the real monk," Kobe jokes.

Carlos laughs, "What? A monk that's about to have a kid."

"Where's Selena?" Dre asks as they enter the living room.

"Right here, Dre," Selena says as she shuffles around the corner. "So good to see you guys.

As Selena hugs them, Carlos looks concerned, "Careful now, babe."

Selena laughs, "You guys have to tell Carlos to ease up on his doting. It's not like the baby is going to drop anytime soon."

"Who knows?" Carlos adds. "The doctor said you will be due soon. Could be anytime, you know."

"Chill, Pops," Noah whispers.

"I need to check the oven," Selena turns to leave.

"Sit, babe. I'll check," Carlos offers.

"You guys are so cute," Dre muses. "I can't wait to have all of these.

"You should try graduating first," Selena smiles.

"That's deep, Dre," Noah adds.

"I agree with Selena, though," Kobe nods, "Dre needs to invest himself in school and sports. This is not the time for you, Dre."

"Says a dude who had a crush on a random girl," Dre smiles.

Carlos enters with dishes of food, "What's that about a random girl Kobe? Have you found the one? Selena and I could help with counseling. These things are harder than you think."

Noah smiles mischievously at Kobe, "Take it from a successful lover and soon-to-be Pops."

Kobe yawns, "Don't mind them Carlos. It's nothing serious."

"Nothing serious?" Dre raises his brow, "It didn't sound like that to me though. There's something about the way she holds her pen."

Noah and Kobe laugh.

"I didn't get that so I'm guessing it's an inside joke," Selena frowns.

"It is. We do it all the time. Sorry Carlos, you don't get in on this one," Dre adds.

Carlos frowns, "Not fair, Dre."

"In the meantime," Dre continues, "I need no invitation to get myself a generous helping of greens. Thank you very much."

"Help yourself, guys," Selena points at the food on the table, "I'll be in the room. If you need anything Carlos is here. I trust him to do a great job of entertaining you guys."

As Selena stands to leave, Carlos gushes, "Easy, babe. You need help?"

"No, Honey. I'm fine," Selena says as she shuffles away.

"When is she due?" Dre asks.

"In a month or two. I am super excited and scared at the same time," Carlos confesses.

"It's expected," Kobe nods. "You do a good job of being a husband, Carlos. I am certain you will be a great dad."

"I hope so," Carlos says.

"So, is it a girl or a boy?" Dre asks.

"Selena didn't want to find out," Carlos sighs.

"How are you gonna get the baby's clothes right?" Noah frowns.

"They may just buy both of 'em," Kobe suggests.

Dre shakes his head, "Hilarious, but it's your choice, Carlos."

Carlos whispers, "I want a boy, though. So he could join the army when he's grown."

"Oh no!" Dre exclaims.

Carlos seems genuinely surprised, "What?"

"You just sounded like your old man, Carlos," Noah confirms. "What if it's a girl?"

"I really haven't figured out that yet," Carlos ponders.

"Well, I hope it's a girl," Dre says under his breath. "We need another beautiful face around."

Carlos grins, "Or another handsome face."

"Say what?" Kobe cups his hand behind his ear.

"Stop yorself Carlos, you aren't that good-looking," Dre laughs.

"Can we just eat in silence?" Carlos tries keeping in his laughter. "We wouldn't want anyone choking on some delicious greens, would we?"

"I don't mind," Dre continues with his dark humor.

"Carlos, when was the last time you spoke to Pops?" Noah asks.

"Some weeks back. Why?" Carlos replies.

"Nothing, just checking. Seems you've settled," Noah adds.

"I thought long and hard about this, you know," Carlos says with a serious face. "Poppa wants the best for me and I understand. I can say that I am not sad that I chose his path."

"Are you happy?" Dre asks.

"I never really thought about it," Carlos grins. "Although I can say I'm in a good place."

"Your Momma?" Kobe asks.

"She's fine. She's been around a couple of times. She's worried about Selena particularly because this birth is close."

Dre shakes his head, "I know nothing about women and childbirth but I know Selena will be fine."

"I know that too," Noah agrees.

"Thanks guys," Carlos looks at his friends.

"Anytime. We got your back," Kobe agrees.

Dre finishes his meal, "Got any beer?"

Carlos smiles slyly, "I do."

"What?" Kobe seems surprised, "You drink…"

Carlos cuts in, "I never told you I was, though. Selena doesn't know. If she does she would scold me."

"Whatever happened to…" Noah starts.

"Scripture says to take a little wine for the belly," Carlos confirms.

"Here we have it," Dre laughs. "I was beginning to wonder when scripture was gonna come in."

Carlos laughs, "I will be right back."

"You said wine but when has beer become wine? Am I missing something?" Dre asks.

"Just see the beer as wine. Noah?" Carlos winks.

Noah smiles, "Water is just fine, Carlos."

Kobe rubs his hands together, "I will drink."

Moments later, Carlos comes back with beer and serves them while he hands over a bottle of water to Noah.

Kobe takes a deep gulp, "Nothing more satisfying than a cold beer."

Dre turns to Noah, "Sure you don't want some?"

"I do!" Noah shakes his head.

"Too bad," Dre opens his can.

Kobe smiles, "I was going to say Noah has been holding up quite well. Dre don't go tempting him. It ain't fair."

"I was kidding, though," Dre adds. "It seems the older we grow the more uptight we become. Don't lose your child's spirit they say. Now I see how age can suck that right outta you."

Carlos shrugs, "I don't think age has anything to do with that. It depends on the person."

"I guess because some are fun-loving than others they take it into old age," Kobe says. "But we can't deny that age comes with maturity and then you realize you have to drop certain things. Life gets more serious as you age."

"I don't totally agree," Noah raises his finger. "Maturity isn't directly proportional to age sometimes. I have seen a lot of old guys who act like they're still kids. Young Marley is still a teenager with the mind of an adult."

"Yeah! I agree with Noah," Carlos adds.

"Both of them are right," Dre speaks up. "Life gets more serious as you age and you just have to seat yourself and talk sense into your head. As you age you realize you have to get your act together."

"Using Carlos as an example," Kobe says, "He is going to be a father soon and there are so many ways he has to man up to be a model for his little one. The fact that he's married has also helped him adjust his lifestyle. He barely even hangs out with us anymore."

"That's not because I don't want to," Carlos protests. "It's because as a married man I have a responsibility to be with my wife. Selena let me hang out with you sometimes."

"It isn't like before," Dre admits.

"Dre!" Noah scolds. "He has new responsibilities now. That's just life."

"Yeah! Life changes you," Kobe agrees.

"It sure does," Dre nods. "Just look at Kobe's pops. Life humbles you at a point."

"How's Kobe's Poppa?" Carlos asks.

"Repentant and proud of his son," Noah beams.

"Wow! That's awesome. How about Reggie and the gang?" Carlos looks towards Kobe.

"Since we moved," Kobe shrugs, "That's the last I heard of him. The news had it that there's a shoot-out at the area and I guess Reggie went down."

Carlos smiles, "Hmm! The end of a street thug."

Dre puts his hands in the air, "Preach, Carlos."

"Guys remember how we had a close shave with..." Noah starts.

"Dude!" Kobe smiles. "My blood ran cold on that night. My black life flashed before my eyes."

"My memory is blurry. Tell me," Dre smiles slyly.

Noah rolls his eyes, "You were drunk, Dre. You and Carlos."

"Carlos never had a high tolerance for alcohol," Dre shrugs. "I guess he was dead drunk after two glasses."

Carlos laughs, "I don't think so. It took more than that to get me drunk. I wasn't really drunk. At least I remember what happened. It's the night of my life."

"To think that we were just a bunch of youth stopped by White cops," Noah continues, "I would have sworn we would've been shot at."

"Man!" Kobe thinks back. "I could barely stand straight. My legs were giving way under me. I had seen my Pop's face. Man! Was he happy to see me behind bars?"

"Yeah! I noticed you had lost it. Panic was written all over you," Noah confirms.

"Noah had the highest level of courage that night. Dude was passing silent messages to me."

"I wasn't courageous inside," Noah admits. "I was trembling."

"I remember us stopping in the middle of the road," Dre muses.

"Everybody remembers that, Dre. With the loud music blaring from our speaker."

"Yeah! The music was crazy," Dre laughs.

"That was the madness that almost made us go to jail," Noah scoffs. "I feared for our lives."

"You know that part where they started the search..."

"And you said shoot!" Dre finishes.

"Funny you remembered that word," Kobe adds.

"See! I wasn't totally down," Dre smiles.

"That jacket had so many pockets and to think they didn't find the stuff still baffles me," Noah muses.

"He got distracted by the mixtape," Kobe rolls his eyes.

"Thank our stars he was a mixtape person," Carlos nods.

"The wave of relief that washed over me," Kobe brushes his hand over his forehead.

"Me too," Noah adds.

"I wonder what my Poppa would have said if that situation had escalated," Carlos thinks aloud.

"He may probably say what a disgrace you are to Santiago's family," Dre offers.

Carlos laughs, "True."

"We got off fairly easy," Kobe pauses. "Much lighter than I would expect."

"That's what a mixtape can do for you," Dre jokes.

"That night I vowed never to allow you guys talk me into any foolish enterprise," Noah confesses.

Kobe agrees, "As did I."

Dre laughs, "It's actually funny. We talked ourselves into that shit. Nobody is innocent. We like it or not, we exhibit same levels of foolishness shockingly at the same time."

Noah checks his watch, "My AA appointment is in about an hour's time."

Dre drains his can and gets up, "All right! We are good to go."

Kobe sips slowly, "Well, I ain't Dre. I can't finish a can of beer comfortably. Thanks, Carlos for having us."

"Anytime, bro," Carlos smiles. "We are brothers, you know that."

Dre raises his voice so Selena can hear him, "Thanks for the food Selena. It's really delicious."

Selena shouts back, "I'm glad you enjoyed yourself! Bye guys. Carlos, don't forget to get me a glass of juice when you come back. I'll be expecting. Don't forget."

Carlos sighs as he walks to the front door to see his friends off, "All right! I won't."